The Secret

WHAT GREAT LEADERS KNOW —AND DO

Ken Blanchard

Mark Miller

BK

BERRETT-KOEHLER PUBLISHERS, INC.
San Francisco

Berrett-Koehler Publishers, Inc.
235 Montgomery Street, Suite 650
San Francisco, CA 94104-2916
Tel: (415) 288-0260 Fax: (415) 362-2512 www.bkconnection.com

ORDERING INFORMATION

Quantity sales. Special discounts are available on quantity purchases by corpora-
tions, associations, and others. For details, contact the "Special Sales Department"
at the Berrett-Koehler address above.

Individual sales. Berrett-Koehler publications are available through most bookstores. They can also be ordered direct from Berrett-Koehler: Tel: (800) 929-2929;
Fax: (802) 864-7626; www.bkconnection.com

Orders for college textbook/course adoption use. Please contact Berrett-
Koehler: Tel: (800) 929-2929; Fax: (802) 864-7626.

Orders by U.S. trade bookstores and wholesalers. Please contact Publishers
Group West, 1700 Fourth Street, Berkeley, CA 94710. Tel: (510) 528-1444; Fax
(510) 528-3444.

Production Management: Michael Bass Associates

Berrett-Koehler and the BK logo are registered trademarks of Berrett-Koehler
Publishers, Inc.

Printed in the United States of America

Berrett-Koehler books are printed on long-lasting acid-free paper. When it is
available, we choose paper that has been manufactured by environmentally responsible processes. These may include using trees grown in sustainable forests, incorporating recycled paper, minimizing chlorine in bleaching, or recycling the energy
produced at the paper mill.

Library of Congress Cataloging-in-Publication Data
Blanchard, Kenneth H.
    The secret: what great leaders know—and do. / Ken Blanchard, Mark Miller.
    p. cm.
    Includes bibliographical references and index.
    ISBN 1-57675-289-5
    1. Leadership. 2. Management. I. Miller, Mark. 1959– II. Title

    HD57.7.B563   2003
    658.4'092—dc22
                                                                    2003063919

First Edition

09 08 07 06 05 04   10 9 8 7 6 5 4 3 2 1

*This book is dedicated to
the next generation of
serving leaders.*

Contents

Foreword

Everything rises and falls on leadership! That's why I've been a student, a practitioner, and an advocate of leadership for more than thirty years. That's also the reason I agreed to write the foreword for this book. When I learned that Ken Blanchard and Mark Miller had collaborated on this project, I knew it would be a winner. Here's why:

Ken has been thinking and writing about leadership for more than a quarter of a century. Just look at this list of titles: *The One Minute Manager®*, *Leadership and the One Minute Manager*, *Gung Ho!*, *High Five!*, *Raving Fans®*, and *Whale Done®!* The list could go on and on, and I'm sure you've heard of many of these books (I hope you've read some of them as well). Ken has sold more than thirteen million books—and counting. He is one of very few authors in history to have four titles on the *Business Week* best-seller list at one time! Ken has helped shape the way our generation leads.

Mark has taken a different path. For more than twenty-five years, he has been part of the leadership team at one of America's great organizations—

Chick-fil-A, Inc., based in Atlanta, Georgia.
Chick-fil-A is a quick-service restaurant company
with more than 1,100 locations and sales approaching $2 billion annually. Currently, Mark serves as
vice president for training and development. I've
had the privilege of speaking at the company's
annual meeting on two occasions, and these people
get it! *The Secret* is no secret in this organization. It
is at the heart of their success.

My challenge to you is simple: learn *The Secret*—
then apply *The Secret*. If you do, your leadership and
your life will be transformed forever!

—John C. Maxwell
Author of
The 21 Irrefutable Laws of Leadership
Founder of The INJOY Group

The Opportunity

How can leadership be this hard? One year ago today was the happiest day of my life. I had arrived! Only four years out of college, and my company had selected me to move into a leadership position: director of corporate client services for the southeast sales region. I knew I could handle the job. I had started out in our catalogue call center fielding customer requests as well as complaints. Then I was promoted to a project manager working closely with sales and our corporate clients. Whatever products or services the salespeople promised our customers, I was supposed to deliver. And if I do say so myself, I was good at getting our corporate clients what they needed, when and where they needed it. I received all kinds of kudos for my ability to develop outstanding client relations. I was sure I could make my staff do the same.

A year ago, I was elated; today, I am holding on for dear life, and my job may be at risk. What happened? What went wrong?

With those thoughts, Debbie pulled into the parking lot at the public library. She knew she could never have an uninterrupted day in the office.

Besides, her boss had always encouraged her to take some time every month to step back and **Assess** what had happened, **Affirm** what was working, and make **Adjustments** as needed. She had always been too busy to actually try it, but today was different. Drastic times demand drastic measures.

As Debbie entered the library, her mind flashed back to long-forgotten memories from her less-than-stellar educational career. The musty smell of the old volumes was as strong as ever. The lighting was about the same—a bit too dark. That had never made much sense to her. *Why aren't libraries better lit?*

Debbie approached the librarian and said, "Hi, I'm looking for a place to work. Somewhere with ample light, if that's possible."

"Certainly," the woman said with a smile. "Are there any particular resources you'll need today?"

"No, but thanks anyway. I just need a quiet place to work for a few hours. I have a few business issues that I need to resolve."

"Let me know if you need any help," the librarian offered. She escorted Debbie to a table in a quiet corner with two large windows on each side.

Debbie took a seat, pulled out her laptop and began. *First, I need to get a firm grip on my current situation. Then I'll try to determine how I got into this mess.*

Current Situation

Feedback from Salespeople	Worst among all 7 sales regions
Customer Satisfaction	Worst among all 7 sales regions

Profit Contribution	Below goal
Cost Management	At goal
Employee Satisfaction	Significantly below where it was when I took over the team.
Turnover	I've lost 4 out of 10 team members in less than a year. This feels like an issue.

Okay, that's where we are today. How did things get so bad, so fast? She thought back over the previous twelve months. Which events might have contributed to her team's current lackluster performance?

Key Events

June 1	I am appointed as team leader.
June 15	First team meeting—conflict over changes I wanted the team to implement.
July	Selected Bob—new to the company—poor decision.
August	Cut expenses to improve profitability.
September	Two new hires: Brenda—good fit; Charles—wait and see.
October	Lost one important client due to poor service from our people.
November	Bob terminated. Team seems very disengaged.

December	Year-end results reflect significant drop in team performance versus previous year.
January	Performance reviews with each member of the team. Every team member is challenged to "step up or step out."
February	Lost two more clients—same reason as before.
May	Team meetings canceled until further notice—focus on improving results.

Wow! No wonder it was a bad year. Look at all the stuff that happened. Unfortunately, I don't think "stuff just happened" is the insight I need to turn things around.

Debbie's somber thought was interrupted by the librarian. "How's your work going? Getting everything done?"

"Not exactly. I've reviewed the current situation, but I don't know where to go from here," Debbie admitted.

"Maybe I can help," the librarian said.

Debbie was amused by the comment but tried not to show it. "Well, thank you, but I'm not sure you could. It's a complex problem."

"Oh, I didn't mean that I could personally help you solve your problem," the woman responded patiently. "However, we do have quite a few resources about business at our disposal. What is the problem you're trying to solve?"

"In our company, we often refer to problems as opportunities," Debbie explained.

"Okay, what's the opportunity?" the woman said with a smile as she continued to probe.

"I think I could sum it up by saying that I have an opportunity to improve the performance of my team."

"Do you know what's causing the performance issues?"

Debbie paused. "I'm not sure. I listed all the key events from the last year and several things that could have contributed, but—"

"But what?" the woman asked.

"I get this sinking feeling that I may be a significant part of the problem. I've only been the team leader for about a year, and I have no prior training or experience." Debbie thought, *I can't believe I'm baring my soul to the librarian.*

"We've got quite a few resources on leadership development," the librarian offered.

"Leadership development," Debbie repeated.

"Yes," said the librarian, "you said you might be part of the problem."

"I think I said I might be a contributing factor, but the real issue is performance." Debbie could feel herself getting defensive. It was one thing to admit she might be part of the problem. It had a different ring to it when she heard someone else say it.

The librarian stepped back. "Okay, I'll leave you alone to work on it yourself."

As the woman walked away, Debbie reconsidered. *Maybe there are some new leadership tricks I can learn.* What could she lose at this point? Only her job and her dream. "Wait!" she called out. "I'm sorry. I was a bit defensive. I've been under a lot of pressure."

The woman turned back with an understanding smile. "It's okay."

"Where are those resources that you mentioned?" Debbie asked, relieved that the librarian was still willing to help.

"Follow me." The librarian led Debbie to a nearby computer, and together they scrolled through the listings, which included titles such as these:

- *The Power of 360-Degree Feedback*
- *Development Plans that Work*
- *Leaders Mentoring Leaders*
- *What Do Leaders Do?*

Debbie began to see something as they scrolled from page to page. The word *mentoring* was repeated several times; in fact, it was repeated on almost every page she reviewed. Then it hit her!

"Excuse me," she said.

She went back to her laptop and opened her e-mail. She was sure she had seen a message that had something to do with mentoring. It read:

Send to: All Supervisors and Managers
From: Melissa Arnold
Subject: Mentoring Opportunities
Date: May 23

As outlined in our annual plan, we indicated that
assisting the current and next generation of leaders
would be one of our top priorities for this year and
for years to come. We believe that one way we
can assist our emerging leaders is to establish a
formal mentoring program within the organization.
We want to be very clear that **this program is
optional.** Any of you who wish to participate need
to submit an application to me before June 1.

If you would like additional information about the
program, there will be a "Lunch and Learn" on
Friday, May 28, in the fourth floor conference room
from 12:15 until 1 P.M. Bring your own lunch.

This could be the ticket, Debbie thought. *I'm sure a
mentor from within the company would help solve the
issues in my area. My mentor will probably be able to
diagnose the problem and tell me how to fix it in a meeting or two. Besides, it might even look good in my per-
sonnel file to say that I was mentored by an executive.*

An alarm went off in Debbie's mind: *Today is the
28th! I've missed the informational meeting. But if I
leave now, I can go by the office and pick up one of those
applications, fill it out this weekend, and submit it
Monday morning before the deadline.*

Debbie gathered her things and headed for the library exit. "Thanks for your help," she called to the librarian on her way out.

"Any time," the woman replied with a smile. "Good luck!"

The Meeting

Debbie worked on the application for several hours over the weekend. It contained all the usual demographic questions but didn't stop there. There were quite a few personal questions and several unexpectedly challenging ones about why she wanted to be in the program. The final question was the one that made her really stop and think.

What is a leader?

Debbie suspected that a good answer to this simple, straightforward question would help her get into the program. She worked for quite some time trying to articulate her reply. She felt she should know the answer because being a leader had long been her primary career objective. Yet she had never given the meaning of leadership much thought. Her first few definitions were, by her own standards, awkward or simplistic. They included:

- A leader is the person in charge.
- A leader is the person in the position that others report to.

* A leader is a person who makes things happen.

Although Debbie believed there was truth in each of these, she was not satisfied. She had an uneasy feeling that there was a correct answer, but she didn't have a clue what it was. It was the same feeling she'd had when it first occurred to her that she might actually be part of her team's performance problems. Nonetheless, it was getting late, and the application needed to be submitted the next morning. Still uncertain, she finally wrote these words:

A leader is a person in a position of authority who is responsible for the results of those under his or her direction.

Early Monday morning Debbie headed straight to Human Resources with her application in hand. She was surprised but pleased to be greeted by the department director, Melissa Arnold.

"Hi, I'm Debbie Brewster, the director of corporate client services from the southeast sales region," she said, extending a hand.

"Yes, Debbie. It's good to see you again," Melissa replied as she shook her hand. "I believe we met at the company picnic a couple of years ago. Do you and your husband still play golf?"

Debbie was amazed. She didn't even remember the picnic from two years ago, let alone meeting Melissa there. *How . . . no, why did she remember*

me or that John and I play golf? I don't even know what
my team members do when they're not at work, much
less remember their spouses' interests.

"You've got a good memory! Yes, we do still play,
although not as much as we used to before I became
a team leader. It seems as though I don't have as
much time these days."

"What brings you to Human Resources so early
on a Monday morning?" Melissa asked.

"I want to submit my application for the mentoring program," Debbie explained.

"Great! Any particular area you're needing help
with?"

"No, I just think that at this point in my career,
I could use a fresh set of eyes to look at my team's
performance."

Melissa frowned. "Our program is not set up as
a consulting arrangement. Its focus is more on the
individual leader and your development. Maybe
you need someone from our internal consulting
division—"

"No," Debbie interrupted. "I guess I could have
stated it better. I need some help. My first year in
leadership has been much more difficult than I
thought it would be. I think a mentor could help."

"Okay, we'll process your application and see if
we can find a good fit. You'll get an e-mail in two
weeks advising you whether you have been selected
to participate in this phase of the program or not.
If you're in, we'll let you know who your mentor
will be."

Debbie felt hopeful. "Sounds great. Thank you for your time."

"My pleasure. I'm here to serve. Let me know if I can help in the future."

How odd that she would say her role is to serve, Debbie thought as she left. *For goodness sakes, she's the head of Human Resources. Someone had better tell her that her role is to lead.*

When Debbie got back to her office, she was immediately reminded of why she needed a mentor. She felt like a firefighter, running from one burning house to another. She knew she should probably be the fire chief calling out orders for her staff to execute, but she realized time and time again that she was the one fighting the fires. Often, her staff would simply bring her the burning issue and step back and let her take care of it. This was the reason why she had less time to play golf. She did her staff's work during the day, and she did her own work on nights and weekends. It was clearly not a sustainable life.

The next two weeks passed in a blur as Debbie waited for word about the mentoring program. The actual situations changed, but it seemed her role never varied. The work—or the way she was going about it—was killing her. When she got home at night, exhausted and frustrated, she would wonder if she had pursued the wrong dream. Maybe leadership was not for her. She hoped a mentor could help. Deep inside, she knew that her future would depend on it.

On the morning she expected word about the mentoring program, Debbie checked her e-mail. No message. She braced for a long, anxious day waiting for the message. But soon she was so involved in solving other people's problems that she had no time to worry about the much-anticipated e-mail.

At lunchtime, Brenda, one of her team members, approached Debbie in the coffee room.

"Can I talk to you about a personal issue?" Brenda asked.

Debbie had noticed that Brenda's performance had slipped somewhat in recent weeks, but she had not taken the time to find out why. She certainly didn't have time now to talk about personal matters.

"I'm sorry, Brenda, maybe later. I'm busy right now." It never crossed Debbie's mind that Brenda's performance and her personal problem could be related. Debbie went into her office and closed the door. As she scanned her new messages, she spotted an e-mail from Melissa. She opened it and read:

Send to: Debbie Brewster
From: Melissa Arnold
Subject: Mentoring Program
Date: June 14

I am pleased to inform you that you have been selected to participate in Phase I of our new Mentoring Program. Your mentor will be Jeff Brown.

Someone from Jeff's office will contact you to
schedule your first meeting. If you have questions,
please let me know.

Debbie thought her heart had stopped. *Surely
there must be a mistake. Jeff Brown is the president of
the company! There is no way he could be my mentor.*

She picked up the phone and placed a call to
Melissa Arnold's office. Melissa's assistant answered
the phone.

"This is Todd. How may I serve you?"

"I'm calling for Melissa Arnold. Is she in?"

"No, I'm sorry, she's at lunch right now. What
can I do for you?"

"Nothing, really," Debbie answered. "I've just
been accepted in the new mentoring program, and
there's been a mistake regarding my mentor."

"Let me check that for you. What is your name?"

"Debbie Brewster."

"Yes, Debbie, I see your name. And your mentor
is—" It felt like a week before Todd finished the
sentence. "Jeff Brown."

"That can't be!" Debbie replied in disbelief.

"Why not?"

"He's the president of the company!"

"That's true," Todd replied.

"Why would Jeff Brown take time to mentor me,
or anybody else?" Debbie asked.

"When you have your first meeting, why don't
you ask him yourself?" Todd suggested.

"I think I will. Thank you for your help."

"My pleasure."

The next day Debbie could still hardly believe that her mentor was the president of the company. Midmorning she received a call from Mr. Brown's assistant.

"Jeff is available on the 22nd in the morning and the 24th in the afternoon. If those times don't work for you, we can go to the week of the 28th. What would work with your schedule? Jeff would like the first meeting to last about an hour, if possible," she said.

Debbie was confused again. *Why is she asking me when it would be convenient for me? Shouldn't the president's schedule take priority over mine?*

Debbie timidly suggested, "How about the 28th?"

"Okay, what time? You choose. Eight, nine, ten, or eleven?"

"Nine sounds good."

"Great. Jeff will see you on June 28 at 9:00 A.M. in his office."

"Thank you, but I've got one more question," Debbie added. "Can you send me any background information on Mr. Brown? I really don't know much about him at all."

"I'll be glad to. You'll get an e-mail later today."

When the e-mail arrived, Debbie was impressed by the efficiency of Mr. Brown's assistant—as well as by the depth of the information she provided. She learned that Mr. Brown was well educated and had a track record of successes at several other companies. He was involved in volunteer work when not pre-occupied by company matters. Debbie also did her own Internet search and discovered that Mr. Brown had written several articles and spoken at numerous colleges and universities. His topic was always the same: leadership.

The night before Debbie's first mentoring meeting, the dinner conversation at home revolved around only one topic.

"I feel like I should be more prepared," Debbie said as she passed the rolls to her husband, John. "It's a special opportunity to meet with the president of the company, and I want to maximize my time."

"You might want to think about some questions you'd like to ask him," John suggested.

"Questions about what?" asked Debbie.

"That's what you need to decide. How many meetings do you get to have with him?"

"I don't know. If he can solve my performance issues in one meeting, that will be fine with me."

John furrowed his brows. "If you could ask him just one question, what would it be?"

Debbie didn't have an immediate answer.

"Well?" John prodded.

"If I could pose only one question, it would be this," said Debbie. 'Mr. Brown, what is the secret of great leaders?'"

The next morning Debbie arrived at Mr. Brown's office a few minutes early.

"Come right in," he said as he greeted her at the door.

"Thank you, Mr. Brown, for meeting with me."

He smiled warmly. "Please, call me Jeff."

"Okay, sir . . . uh . . . Jeff. As I was saying, thank you for meeting with me today," Debbie stammered slightly.

"Please, have a seat," Jeff offered.

Debbie pulled out the chair in front of his desk, but he redirected her to a chair in a small seating area on the other side of the room. He joined her there.

She couldn't help but notice that although it was a nice office, it wasn't very large, nor was it extravagantly furnished. She had expected something more stately for the president's office. She did notice one thing that seemed a bit odd: he had a large whiteboard on the wall.

Jeff began the conversation. "I'm excited about our time together. I love working with young leaders."

"I'm excited, too, but don't you have more important things to do?" Debbie asked.

"I believe that developing leaders is our highest strategic priority as an organization. Everything rises and falls on leadership. If I don't invest time in helping other leaders grow and develop, then the people I work with won't see it as a priority, and they won't invest the time, either. I believe

Everything rises and falls on leadership.

we demonstrate our priorities with the way we allocate our resources—and that includes our time. So, I am delighted to have you as my first mentee in our new program." Once again he gave her a warm smile.

"I think we should meet for an hour about every four to six weeks," Jeff continued. "If we run out of things to say, we'll finish early. If we think we need more time, we can work on the schedule together. Most of the time, we'll conclude our sessions with a homework assignment."

"Homework?" Debbie asked.

"Yes, sometimes I'll have an activity for you and, other times, questions for you to consider between our meetings. For today, let's get to know each other. I'll begin by telling you a little about my background."

Over the next twenty minutes, Debbie learned more about Jeff than all of her research had revealed. He was a fascinating, well-rounded person. "Now tell me about yourself," said Jeff.

She began by telling him about her work over the previous five years at the company. He listened attentively as she talked. She determined very early on that he was a great listener. After a few minutes she wrapped it up. "And that's pretty much all about me."

"Thank you for sharing all of those things about your work," Jeff said. "Now, tell me about your family and your interests outside work."

Debbie wasn't sure why he wanted to know these things, but she did as he requested. He asked several additional questions that made it seem as though he was really interested. When Debbie finally finished, she said, "Is there anything else you'd like to know?"

"How do you think I can best serve you in the months ahead?" Jeff asked.

Debbie confessed that she was not quite sure. She told him some of the challenges her team was experiencing. Again, he listened very carefully and even jotted down a few notes. After she did her best to summarize her situation, she asked, "What suggestions do you have?"

"I'm not sure I'll have a lot of suggestions for you, Debbie. What I can promise you is that over the next few months, you'll find the answers to many of your questions. And looking at the clock, we probably have time for only one more question today."

"I understand. And I decided that if I could only ask one question, I knew what it would be."

"And what's that?" Jeff asked.

"What is the secret of great leaders?"

He smiled. "That's an outstanding question— and a big one. I'm afraid that's more than I want to tackle in the time we have remaining. How about we look at that next time? We'll invest our time in several meetings to help you learn not only the secret of great leaders but how to apply it in your work—and in your life."

Debbie was disappointed. She had hoped that Jeff would have a simple answer and that he could help solve her problem *today*. Yet she was intrigued by his promise to reveal the secret and glad that he seemed genuinely committed to helping her succeed as a leader.

She stood to go. "Thanks again for your time. I look forward to hearing more about the secret at our next meeting!"

The Secret

That night John met Debbie at the door when she got home.

"How was it?" he asked excitedly.

"I'm sorry I forgot to call you," she replied in a stressed tone that spoke volumes about her day. "The meeting was very good. But when I got back to my office, the place was on fire and I didn't have a moment to call."

"What advice did he give you?"

"None yet."

"Nothing?" John asked in disbelief.

"Nope. He said he wanted to get to know me and give me a chance to know him. He said we would have time in the months ahead to find the answer to my question."

"So you asked him your question?" John wondered.

"Yes. He said it was an outstanding question, and we would explore it in future meetings."

"So you spent how long getting to know each other?"

"Almost an hour," Debbie said.

"Wow! What did you learn?"

"I reached two conclusions based on today's meeting," Debbie said. "One, Jeff is a good listener. And two, I know very little about the people on my team."

"What impressed you about his listening skills?" John asked.

"I'm not exactly sure. It seemed as though he was constantly asking me questions that revolved around me and my perspective."

John admitted that he didn't know many people who exhibited that type of listening behavior. "In fact, it seems that most people are so busy thinking about what they want to say next, they really can't hear what you are saying."

"Jeff was different," Debbie replied. "I think that's why I said he's a good listener."

"When is your next meeting?"

"Next month. Between now and then, I'm going to work hard on my listening skills and see what I can learn about my people."

"Sounds like a good plan," John said enthusiastically.

The next morning Debbie went to the office determined to execute her plan. She started with Brenda. She thought this would be difficult initially—on two fronts. First, Debbie wondered whether she would be able to listen—truly listen. Second, she feared Brenda would be suspicious of her sudden change in behavior. But she had been so impressed by her time with Jeff that she decided to forge ahead anyway.

"Brenda, a few days ago you approached me to talk about a personal issue, and I told you I didn't have time. I'm sorry I didn't make the time. Can we have lunch together today?"

Brenda frowned. "Are you sure you're available? If not, I understand. You're always so busy and all."

"Let's do it today," Debbie insisted.

Debbie did her best to listen to Brenda over lunch. She discovered that Brenda's son had been ill for several weeks, and this had contributed to some of the performance issues Debbie had noticed. Brenda asked about the possibility of a more flexible schedule until her son was well. Debbie assured her that they could make this happen.

Debbie continued to work on her listening skills, determined to learn more about her people. Although this was her goal, she quickly became consumed by firefighting again and didn't have much time for listening.

The days moved quickly due to the frantic pace in Debbie's life. Even in the midst of her crazy workdays, she noticed that the flexible schedule was helping Brenda. But despite that improvement, the team's overall performance still did not improve. The only ray of hope on the horizon was Debbie's upcoming meeting with Jeff. In this next meeting,

they would explore the answer to her question—
and hopefully solve some of her team's performance
issues.

The day of her next mentoring meeting finally
arrived. Debbie was pleased with herself for being
punctual. As she had expected, Jeff arrived on time
as well.

"How have things been going since our first
meeting?" Jeff asked.

"Okay, I guess. My team still has performance
issues. I've been working on becoming a better listener, and I've also tried to get to know more about
my people as individuals."

"All good things to do!" Jeff encouraged her with
a smile. "Where should we start today?" he asked.

"I assumed there would be a format that we
would follow," Debbie said. "But if there's not, we
could start with my question."

"Yes, your question about the secret of great
leaders. As I told you at the conclusion of our last
meeting, I think it's a very good question. But before
we go any further, why do you want to know?"

"So I can be a great leader," Debbie replied
without hesitation.

"I read your answer to the question 'What is a
leader?' from your application. As I recall, you said
that 'a leader is a person in a position of authority
who is responsible for the results of those under his
or her direction.'

"In reality, Debbie, true leadership has nothing to do with one's level in the organization. There are

True leader-ship has nothing to do with one's level in the or-ganization.

many individuals in the world who don't hold leadership positions, yet they're providing leadership all the time, just as there are many others who hold leadership positions, and they are not exerting much leadership at all."

The latter case was painful to Debbie because she knew Jeff easily could be talking about her. She was in a *position* of leadership, but based on her team's performance, she evidently was not providing much leadership.

Debbie hesitated for a moment, then asked, "If it's not position, what is leadership?"

"Let me explain it with a picture," Jeff said as he walked over to the whiteboard. "Leadership is a lot like an iceberg. There are two primary components. What you can see above the waterline and what you can't see, below the water. Let's see if you remember this concept from your fifth grade science class. How much of an iceberg is usually visible above the water?"

Debbie thought for a moment. "I think I was out the day we studied icebergs." They both laughed. "I would guess that less than 20 percent of an iceberg is visible above the water," she said.

"That's a good guess. The same principle applies to leadership. Leadership is more about what others don't see than what they do see."

Debbie was starting to feel lost in this explanation. "Keep talking," she said.

"Let's label what we've just discussed," said Jeff as he began to draw on the whiteboard. "Below the water is the character of a leader. Above the water are the skills of a leader. Another way to think about it is that leadership has two components—Being and Doing.

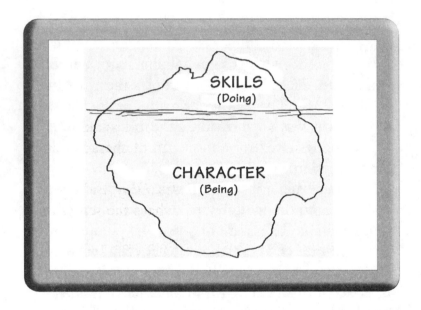

"Think back a hundred years. When ships sailed in northern seas, many fell prey to icebergs. In most of those tragedies, what sunk the ships? The part of the iceberg that was visible—or the part that was under the water, unseen?"

Debbie said, "It was probably what was under the water."

"Exactly," Jeff responded. "Character—or lack of it—is still the nemesis of most leaders in our world today. Skills are critical to effective leadership, but character is also. Many believe they can become effective leaders if they only had the skills. Others believe they can become great leaders if they could just develop their character. Both are wrong. It takes skills and character."

"I see," said Debbie.

"As an organization, where possible we select people with both character and skills. But if we have to choose between skills and character, we've made a fundamental decision on this issue. It's the reason you're here today."

"And what is that decision?" Debbie asked.

"We will select men and women of character and develop their skills."

Debbie made a few quick notes. *Okay, we're getting close*, she thought. "So, Jeff, what's the secret of great leaders?" she asked.

"The secret is, great leaders **SERVE**." Jeff paused to let his words sink in.

"*Serve?* What do you mean by that?" Debbie's tone clearly reflected her disbelief. "Leaders don't serve, they lead! And what does that have to do with an iceberg?"

"The idea of SERVE fits nicely within the metaphor of the iceberg. Let me explain. A leader's motivation or intention is a character issue. Leaders—regardless of their skill level—must continuously ask themselves, 'Why am I leading?'

If I am leading with the intention to serve my people and my organization, I will behave in a fundamentally different way than if my motivation is self-serving. A key question you must continuously ask yourself is 'Am I a serving leader or a self-serving leader?'"

A key question you must continuously ask yourself is "Am I a serving leader or a self-serving leader?"

"I'm confused," Debbie said in a moment of complete candor. "I'm having trouble translating this warm, fuzzy idea of SERVE back to my team. Assuming my motives are good, how do I go about leading?"

"That's where I want us to spend our time over the next few months. Together we're going to explore how the idea of SERVE can and should impact what you *do* as a leader. I trust that those who selected you to be a leader thought you had a servant heart. Otherwise, they would not have asked you to assume a leadership role. So through this mentoring process, our focus will be on your leadership skills and exploring ways you can serve your team and this organization on a day-by-day basis."

"I appreciate your confidence in me, but serving still seems like a big idea. In fact, I think I could spend my lifetime trying to figure out how to serve."

"You're right. I think we just had a breakthrough!" Jeff exclaimed.

"What did I say? What did I break through?" Debbie asked.

"You said you could spend your entire life figuring this out. That's exactly right. Great leaders don't become great in a moment—or in a month or a year. They become great leaders one day at a time throughout their lifetimes. You'll never finish. You'll never completely arrive. You'll constantly and continuously find new ways to serve, and every time you do, your leadership skills will improve and you'll become a better leader."

"This seems overwhelming. There must be millions of things a leader can do to serve."

"You're right. There are millions, but there is also a short list."

"A short list?" There was a degree of hope in Debbie's voice.

"Yes, I believe there are five fundamental ways in which every great leader serves."

Debbie grabbed her pen. "What are they?"

"We'll address them one at a time, beginning with our next meeting," Jeff said. "Today, I want to give you your first assignment. Between now and our next meeting, see how you can serve those you lead. Not just big things, but in all the little ways as well. Keep a list, and we'll talk about it next time we meet."

Debbie left Jeff's office with many unanswered questions, but she also had an intuitive sense that she would never view her role as a leader in the same way again.

Where Are You Going?

Over the next few weeks Debbie worked very hard to serve her team members, although she was not always sure how to do so. Even though many of her attempts seemed insignificant, she could sense a change in her approach to her leadership responsibility and possibly even a change in the team. She made a list of her experiences to share with Jeff at their next meeting.

One of her encounters was particularly note-worthy. Charles was still hanging on for dear life. His performance had improved only slightly since his first month. Debbie felt it would probably be only a few months before she would be forced to let him go. She decided to meet with Charles, ask some open-ended questions, and look for ways to serve him.

"Hello, Charles," Debbie said as she walked into his office.

"To what do I owe this unexpected visit?" Charles asked, somewhat sarcastically.

"I wondered if we could talk for a few minutes."

"Absolutely. What would you like to talk about?"

Debbie wanted to get his full attention. "As we've discussed before, I'm concerned about your performance."

"Yes, I know. You've told me."

"Here's a question I don't think I've asked: How can I help?"

"That *is* a different question," Charles said as he sat up a little straighter in his chair.

"What do you think your greatest challenge is?" Debbie had her own opinion, but she needed to hear his response.

"I know my greatest challenge." Charles let out a deep sigh. "No matter what I do, I can't keep our salespeople or our clients satisfied. Maybe I'm just not organized enough for this job. I work hard, but somehow things get mixed up. Our customers might get what they want but not get it when or where they want it. Other times, they don't even get what they want. I've annoyed some clients so much that we've lost their business. It's like my worst nightmare—I'm a project manager who can't manage projects."

Debbie could tell from listening to Charles that he really cared and wanted to serve. His intentions were good. His project management skills needed some work.

Debbie thought for a moment. "Okay, Charles, here's an idea. When I was in your role, I was a good project manager. If you'd like, I'll work with you for a few days to see where you may be going wrong. I'll even take a few calls for you so you can watch me, if you think that would help."

"You're kidding, aren't you? You would work side by side with me? Why?"

"I want to do everything I can to help you succeed."

Charles was beaming. "Let's do it! When are you available?"

"I believe I can make time next Thursday and Friday. Would that work for you?"

Charles assured Debbie that he would make it work.

Debbie wasn't certain, but when the conversation was over, she felt as though she was beginning to understand the idea behind SERVE.

It wasn't long until Debbie was scheduled to meet with Jeff again. She was excited to share the ways she had been able to serve since their last meeting.

"Good morning, Jeff," she said as she walked in carrying a box of his favorite donuts.

"How did you know?" Jeff asked.

Debbie smiled. "I'm learning to listen and observe more carefully," she said.

"Thank you, Debbie. That was very thoughtful."

"Jeff, you were right. I discovered that I could serve people regardless of my position in the organization. I made a list just as you requested."

"Wonderful! Let's take a look."

"I bought coffee for my staff. I picked up trash in the parking lot on my way into the office the other day. I listened to two of my team members who wanted to talk about personal problems. I've agreed to work with Charles on his skill development as a project manager. There were others, but I think I'm beginning to get it."

"How's your team's performance?" asked Jeff.

"No significant improvement," Debbie said in a tone that revealed her sense of hopelessness.

"Don't worry," Jeff said. "I believe you are beginning to get it. Keep looking for ways to serve your people. However, there's something else you need to know. By themselves, these good behaviors will not make you a great leader. A nicer person to work with, yes—a great leader, no."

"I'm confused again. I thought you said I was supposed to serve," Debbie protested.

"That's right," Jeff affirmed.

"In countless ways," she said.

"Exactly," Jeff agreed.

"And I did."

"Yes, you're right, you did serve. And you need to keep serving because the more you serve, the more you will want to serve. But there's more. Remember in our last meeting I said that there was a short list of things that all great leaders do? Some of the things you did, including picking up trash and buying coffee, aren't on the short list."

Debbie said, "I don't understand."

"You will," Jeff said optimistically. "Your willingness to serve in small ways is another indication that your heart is ready to discover more strategic ways to serve."

"I think I'm ready," Debbie said cautiously, since she had no idea what "more strategic ways to serve" meant.

Jeff walked to the whiteboard and drew the iceberg again. This time he labeled the part above the water with the word *SERVE*.

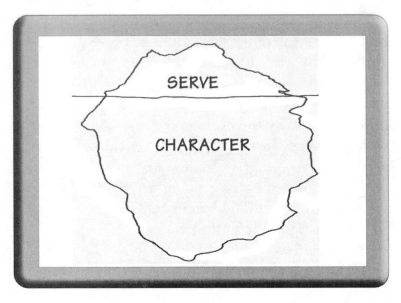

"I've created this simple acronym, SERVE, to help me remember the five key practices of great leaders—the five ways I must serve if I want to reach my full potential as a leader," he said. "These are the things people see. Today, we'll talk about the *S*. We'll explore the others in future meetings. Now, I have a very important question for you. Where are you going with your team?"

"What do you mean?" Debbie had not thought about this before.

"What are you trying to accomplish?"

"I want our salespeople and customers to feel satisfied." Debbie felt this was a safe and valid response.

"Is that all?"

"Isn't that enough?" Debbie asked.

"I'm not sure satisfying our salespeople and customers is very compelling. The *S* stands for **See the Future.** It's about your vision as a leader for the future of your group." Jeff erased the iceberg and wrote on the whiteboard.

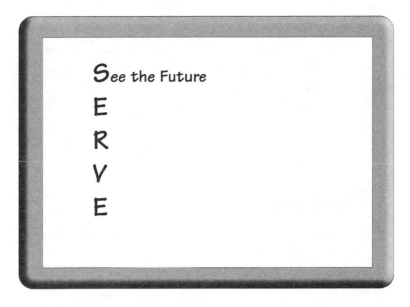

See the Future

E

R

V

E

"A compelling vision stirs passion within you. It tells everyone who works with you who you are, where you're going, and what will drive your behavior. Are you passionate about satisfying your salespeople and customers?"

"It would be nice," Debbie said with a shrug.

"That's my point. If you aren't passionate about something out there in the future—if it doesn't fire you up and get you out of bed in the morning—you can bet your team is not going to be passionate, either.

"A number of years ago, when everyone was going to self-service gasoline stations, a friend of mine decided he would go into the full-service business. He loved to go where there was no competition. He decided that people didn't go to gas stations because they wanted to but because they had to. As a result, they wanted to be in and out of there as quickly as possible. So his vision was to create gas stations that made filling up fast and fun. If you drove into one of his stations, it would be like going to an Indy 500 pit stop. He hired mothers and retirees who were interested in working part-time to make a little extra money and then dressed them in red jumpsuits. When you drove into one of his stations, people would race toward your car and pump your gas, look under your hood, clean your windows, and take your money or credit card—faster than anyone could imagine. The values that drove everyone's behavior were safety, speed, and fun. As you drove away, they would give you a business card that said, 'P.S. We also sell gas.'"

"That certainly sounds fun," said Debbie.

"It sure was," said Jeff. "Leadership is about taking people from one place to another. One of a leader's top priorities must be to assure that the team knows where you are headed. My friend had a clear vision for a different kind of gas station. His people and his customers knew it. Seeing the future is about creating a compelling vision. It is one of the privileges and most serious demands of leaders. It may sometimes be difficult to determine where the enterprise should be heading, but heading somewhere is a must. Envisioning and communicating a future-oriented vision is a huge part of leadership."

Creating a compelling vision is one of the privileges and most serious demands of leaders.

"Are goals and strategies part of the future?" asked Debbie.

"Absolutely," said Jeff. "They take on real meaning when they are in the context of a compelling vision."

Debbie said, "I never thought about that part of leadership. I guess I've been thinking too much about today and very little about the future and where we should be headed."

Jeff nodded. "There is a constant tension between those two in the mind of a leader. I often refer to it as the 'Heads Up versus Heads Down' challenge."

Debbie said, "I think I know where you're going with this, but I would rather not make any assumptions. Please tell me more."

"For example, this discussion is a 'Heads Up' activity because we're talking about vision and direction. Leaders will always need to devote some visioning time to seeing the future because we need to communicate to our people where we are going as well as anticipate opportunities and obstacles. At the same time, we need to help people with implementation—making the vision a reality. That's 'Heads Down.' Leaders must constantly evaluate how they invest their time. Some time must be devoted to Heads Up, and some must be devoted to Heads Down."

"I've got a question," Debbie said. "Do you as a leader have to do all the Heads Up work by yourself?"

"No," said Jeff. "Involving your people will get their commitment. But it's your responsibility to make sure that the Heads Up work gets done. Does that help?"

"Yes, thanks," said Debbie. "You suggested earlier that values should drive everyone's behavior when implementing your vision and future thinking. Do we—I mean, our company—have values?"

"Yes and no," Jeff said.

"That's helpful," Debbie joked. "What does 'yes and no' mean?"

"Our values do exist. Every organization has them. Either they can be created on purpose by leadership, or they will emerge on their own. Regardless of how they are developed, there are always core operating values. Because our organization has never formally articulated them, we are missing a huge opportunity."

"How so?"

"If the values are published, they can be repeated, recognized, and rewarded, with positive results. Since I'm still relatively new to the company, I decided to spend a few months observing the culture to see what values were already in place, as well as what values we may want to incorporate

in the future. Before going public with any new
values that I believe should shape our behaviors,
I wanted to make certain that they were all ground-
ed in some truth and some sense of reality. If not,
we would lose credibility.

Values

are the

beliefs that

drive our

behavior.

"Our values will be featured at
our upcoming annual meeting,"
Jeff added. "You'll also see a lot of
other things reinforcing them in
the months and years to come.
Values are a big deal. They are
the cornerstones of the culture
the leader is trying to create.
Remember this: Our values are
the beliefs that drive our behavior."

Debbie nodded thoughtfully. "I suppose that's
true. What are our values?"

"You can read about our values in our annual
report, which is scheduled to be released next week.
Take a look and let me know what you think."

"Okay, I will," said Debbie.

"When is your next team meeting?" Jeff asked.

"We don't have team meetings any more," she
replied.

"You don't?" Jeff was surprised but tried not to
show it.

"No, I canceled them several months ago,
because performance was so bad. I didn't want to
waste time in meetings when people could be taking
care of clients."

"Interesting. I'd like to talk more about that in a future session. In the meantime, let me give you a few questions to consider. You may be tempted to answer them all yourself, but I'm guessing you'll need to talk to some of your team members."

"I'm ready. Let me have them." As Jeff posed the thought-provoking questions, Debbie jotted them down:

- What is the purpose of your team?
- Where do you want your team to be in five years?
- How many members of your team could tell you what the team is trying to become/achieve?
- What values do you want to drive the behavior of your team?
- How can you communicate your vision of the future to your team?

"These should give you something to think about before our next meeting," Jeff said.

"You're not kidding. I'll be spending more than a little time working on this."

"You're catching on. Great leaders are always asking questions like these—and others that we'll discuss in future meetings. See you in a few weeks."

Debbie left Jeff's office knowing that she was learning the secret of great leaders. But one big question weighed on her. Could she become a great leader? She was cautiously optimistic.

What's Most Important?

Debbie began the new week by working on the questions Jeff had given her. She knew she had not done a good job of Seeing the Future. The only future she was pursuing was keeping up with the sales folks and the client needs. While she knew these were important concerns, she recognized that the SERVE model Jeff had described represented a higher level of thinking and a higher level of leadership.

Numerous leaders who were able to See the Future and provide direction came to Debbie's mind. Many were historical figures: John F. Kennedy and his desire to put a man on the moon; Martin Luther King Jr. and his dream of harmony among people of all racial backgrounds; Mother Teresa and her vision of comfort for the suffering people of India.

As she thought about creating a compelling vision, Debbie remembered one of Jeff's first presentations after he arrived at the company. In that talk, he stated his belief that their business was not about selling—it was about serving the customers and meeting their needs. *Serving?*

He talks about serving all the time. And now, he's teaching me that great leaders SERVE. Interesting!

She wanted to answer all the questions Jeff had given her. She was not very far along in this process when Jennifer, one of her team members, showed up at her door with a problem.

Debbie's first reaction was to deal with it immediately. But she stopped and thought for a moment. *Does this really require my involvement? Can Jennifer solve this on her own?* She knew that if she got involved, she would once again be prevented from thinking about the future. She realized that part of her leadership problem was that she was so consumed with the Heads Down issues of today that she had little, if any, time for Heads Up work on tomorrow. All of these thoughts flashed through her mind in an instant.

"What do you think you should do?" Debbie asked.

Jennifer was caught off guard. "Well . . . I don't know. You usually decide these things."

"Do you think you have all the information you need to make a recommendation?"

"I think so."

"Come back after lunch and let me know what you think we should do. If you need additional information from me, we can talk then."

Jennifer left, looking somewhat in shock.

Debbie returned to her desk with a sense that she had just made a significant step on her leadership journey. She once again turned her attention to the questions about the future.

Where do I want my team to be in five years? As she considered the question, she was reminded that she didn't really have a team. She had abandoned the team concept. What she had now was a group of individuals working independently. There were no opportunities for synergy, shared learning, encouragement, team accountability, or any of the other benefits of working together. She had never taken the time to think about that before now.

Debbie's first action item was to reinstate the team. Together they could not only answer Jeff's questions but also chart their own course to accomplish whatever they set their minds to do.

When the morning mail arrived, the annual report was in the stack. She could hardly wait to see what Jeff had written about the company's values. She opened the report to the president's letter and skimmed quickly to the section on values.

How Do We Ensure Our Future Success?

How will we achieve outstanding financial return and long-standing, mutually beneficial relationships? I believe we will do this by incorporating and living by a number of core values. As you review the following, you will find very little new or different. During my short time in this organization, I have seen countless examples of men and women living these values. My intent in publishing them here is to highlight them and declare publicly: These are the beliefs that will guide our behavior and ensure our continuing success.

Customers First

Customers are the reason each of us has a job. Our thoughts and actions should always be focused on answering the question "How will this decision or action impact the customer?" We will continue to put customers first in our priorities and our decision making.

Serve Others

We have enjoyed success in the past because of the willingness of our people to serve. As we serve others, we almost always reap the rewards. Not that our motive to serve is to get—that's just how it tends to work out in the end. I believe that *those who wish to become great must be willing to serve.* We will continue to be an organization known for our "servant spirit."

Stewardship

A *steward* is someone who is enlisted by an owner and charged with the management of the owner's possessions. I believe that all the things we have at our disposal are on loan. We can't take them with us, but we can use them while we're here on Earth. I also believe that we are accountable for all that has been entrusted to us—our time, talents, financial resources, and relationships. We will act accordingly. We will continue to be good stewards.

Creativity

This has been—and will always be—a hallmark of our organization. We will value creativity, recognize it, recruit people who have it, and develop it in those where it is latent. The ability to think creatively is a gift we've all been given, and we are determined to utilize it to the fullest. We will never be satisfied with the status quo.

You'll hear much more about these values in the months and years to come. To our employees—our team—thank you for living them every day. To our shareholders, thank you for your confidence in us.

It is my privilege to serve you!

Jeff Brown

President & Chief Operating Officer

As Debbie finished reading the letter, she felt proud to be part of her organization. She was thankful for the time she had spent with Jeff and could hardly wait for their next meeting. In the days that followed, Debbie realized that old habits were hard to break. On several occasions, she found herself engaged in all-too-familiar activities: specifically, fighting fires and making decisions that others should or could make. However, she didn't do these things quite as often, and when she was able to restrain herself, she found that she had more time to think about the questions from her last meeting with Jeff. The more she worked on them, the more excited she became. She felt as though the picture of the future she was creating was generating some passion in her. Plus, as she began to share her vision, she found others wanting to get in on the action as well.

Debbie talked with each member of her team. With their help she was able to develop at least a partial answer to each of Jeff's questions about Seeing the Future. She was eager to share her insights and progress with him.

The day of their next mentoring meeting finally arrived. As Debbie approached Jeff's office, she was greeted by his assistant. "Jeff will be about five minutes late this morning. May I get you some coffee?"

"No, thank you." As Debbie waited, she enjoyed the rare moments of peace and quiet. Minutes later Jeff walked in and hung up his coat.

"I apologize for being late," he said. "I always try to be punctual. For me, it's about honoring other people's time. I'm very sorry, but I was finishing up an interview with a candidate for one of our new positions. It was our fourth and final meeting. I think we're getting close to a decision."

"You've had four interviews with the same candidate?" Debbie asked in a tone of disbelief.

"Yes. Why does that surprise you?"

"I usually spend thirty minutes with a potential employee."

Jeff made a mental note of her comment and said, "I look forward to hearing about your thought process on that at a future meeting. For now I'd like you to give me a quick report on what you've done since our last meeting."

"First, let me congratulate you on your letter in the annual report!" Debbie said with enthusiasm. "It confirmed to me why I'm so committed to this organization."

"Thanks," Jeff said. "What have you learned since our last meeting that will help you and your team accomplish your vision?"

"Two big things come to mind," Debbie replied. "First, I've tried to delegate more so that I can have time to think about the future. You really opened my eyes to my responsibility to do that. I realized that if I'm not thinking about creating the future, probably no one else on the team is going to do it."

"Yes," Jeff replied, adding, "It's been said that seeing the future is one leadership responsibility that cannot be delegated. It can be shared, but it's the leader's job to make time today to ensure that there is a tomorrow."

It's the leader's job to make time today to ensure that there is a tomorrow.

"The second breakthrough is that I've decided to reinstate the team. I realized that the advantages far outweigh the disadvantages and that we are much more likely to achieve our desired future if we work together."

"It sounds like it was a big month for you. Anything else?" Jeff asked.

"I talked with the team members about your questions. We have some initial thoughts on all of them, but we will continue to refine the answers in the days ahead."

"Let's take a look at what you have," Jeff said.

They spent the next few minutes reviewing Debbie's work. As always, Jeff listened intently and periodically stopped her to ask a thought-provoking question or two. Debbie was unable to give an immediate response to most of his questions, but she took careful notes.

"Let's use the remaining time this morning to talk about your team," Jeff said.

"I thought we were going to talk about the *E* in the SERVE model," Debbie protested politely.

"We are," said Jeff as he walked over to the whiteboard and wrote next to the *E*.

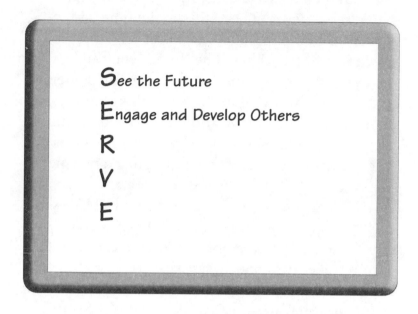

See the Future

Engage and Develop Others

R

V

E

"As you can see, the *E* is for **Engage and Develop Others**," Jeff continued. "Here's what I mean by that. You must have the right people, in the right roles, fully engaged if you are going to accomplish the things you identified under See the Future. Everything that you will accomplish as a leader ultimately hinges on the people you have around you. Without this piece, your success as a leader will be greatly limited."

"Tell me what you mean by Engage," Debbie said with a curious look on her face.

"Gladly. To me, Engage has two distinct components. The first has to do with selection. If we do

not select the right people for the right job, we have
made a serious leadership error."

"And then we have to fix it," Debbie added.

"Yes, but never underestimate the time and
energy necessary to 'fix it.' The costs of a poor
selection are staggering. The 'fix,' as you call it,
requires time, mental energy, and emotional energy.
And while we're fixing it, there are almost always
other costs to the organization: the cost of declining
performance and missed opportunities, as well as the
cost of recruiting, selecting and training a new person. And don't forget the cost to morale."

"What exactly do you mean by that?" Debbie asked.

Jeff's expression was serious. "Other people
suffer when a poor performer is on the team. The
team members will not always step up and say it,
but it does impact them. They can easily become
discouraged."

"I've seen that happen," Debbie offered.

Jeff nodded. "As leaders, if we do not own up to
our bad decisions and rectify the situation, we lose
credibility with our people. Yet it's not always easy
for the leader to admit the mistake and take the
needed corrective action. That's why the best leaders work diligently to select good people. It's also
why I just completed my fourth interview with a
candidate."

"Are four interviews really necessary?" Debbie
asked.

"Most of the time, yes. Not only have we
got to be sure about the candidate, we want him

or her to be sure about us. One of the things I do with all candidates is to give them ample time to interview me during the process."

This idea sounded very foreign to Debbie. "Interview you?"

"Yes, I always allocate time for them to ask me any questions they may have about me, the job, or the organization. You can learn a lot about people by the questions they ask. So it's really a win-win situation. They learn what they need to know to make a good decision, and so do I. I want both of us to get as many of our questions answered as possible, before I add them to my team."

"That's a great idea," Debbie said.

"There's one more part of the process," Jeff added.

"What else can you possibly do?" Debbie asked in disbelief.

"I give candidates a copy of my personal and professional references so they can check me out. I'm going to check their references, so why not let them check mine?"

Debbie could not believe what she was hearing. In most cases, she spent less than half an hour with her candidates. She had not been treating this part of her leadership responsibility with the seriousness Jeff seemed to believe it deserved. Maybe this was the answer to her high turnover problem.

"Anything else?" Debbie asked, half jokingly.

Jeff thought for a moment. "Yes, there is. I always spend some time during the last interview trying to talk the candidate out of taking the job."

"You've got to be kidding! After all you have invested in the process, I would think you would be trying to close the sale."

"If I can talk candidates out of accepting the job, they don't need to join our team. I would rather have them decide now they don't want to work here rather than six months or a year from now. I would rather lose a candidate than a team member."

"I'll need to think about this for a while," Debbie confessed.

"Good. Let me give you one quote to consider. It's from Peter Drucker, the management and leadership guru. He was asked, 'What is the most important decision an executive makes?' He responded, 'Who does what.' Getting the right people in the right jobs is the first part of the term Engage.

With every pair of hands you hire, you get a free brain.

"Another part of Engage has to do with the level of buy-in people have for a cause, their work, and a leader. You want to do more than enlist their hands—you want to engage their heads and hearts also. I often say that with every pair of hands you hire, you get a free brain. Unfortunately, many leaders operate as if that were not true. It's as if they have a large sign that hangs over the front door of their business that says:

> **Check your brains at the door. They will be returned to you as you leave the building.**
>
> —The Management

"Although I've never actually seen a sign like this, I see leaders treat their people this way in businesses large and small all over the world. It's a tragedy! The wasted human potential is incalculable. Great leaders don't tolerate this type of environment."

Debbie could sense Jeff's intense passion on this particular issue.

He continued, "The only way to get the use of these free brains is to engage people in the cause and the work. And when you get their brains, you can often get their hearts as well. Then you've really got something!

"One of my favorite historical examples of this is the story of Spartacus. He was a slave who led an uprising against the Roman government. If you've ever seen the movie, you probably remember the scene near the end when the slaves had been captured by the Romans. The Roman general tells them that if they reveal Spartacus to him, he will spare their lives. At that moment, Spartacus stands and says, 'I am Spartacus.' Unexpectedly, the slave next to him stands and says, 'I am Spartacus.' And then the next one does the same thing, and the next, until the entire legion is standing."

"I've seen the movie," said Debbie. "It's quite an inspiring scene."

"That's one of our primary challenges as leaders," said Jeff. "To create levels of engagement such that when we, as leaders, stand on an issue, our people will stand with us."

"But how do you engage people like that?" Debbie asked.

"We may not always engage them to the extent Spartacus did," Jeff acknowledged with a smile. "However, we all have a tremendous opportunity to capture the hearts and minds of our people. As a leader, you'll invest a huge part of your life trying to figure out how to do that."

"Could you explain that more?" asked Debbie.

"Let me ask you, what are the things that fire you up about your work? What are the conditions that led you in the past to be fully engaged?"

Debbie was silent for a moment. "As I think back to the times when I was really involved in my work, a few things come to mind."

Jeff said, "Write them on the board. I find that it often helps me to see in writing what I'm thinking."

Debbie stepped up, erased the whiteboard and wrote:

- My goals were clear.
- I was well trained.
- I had the information I needed.
- My boss had confidence in me.
- My boss was there when I needed help.
- I was making a contribution.
- We were all learning and growing.

With that, she sat down and looked at the list. Her memories of those days were wonderful.

Jeff said, "It appears that you know exactly what an engaging environment looks like. I'll bet I can add a couple other things you didn't mention. First, I'm guessing your boundaries were pretty clear."

"Yes," Debbie agreed. "I knew what they were when the project began. All the team members did."

"And you were also expected to think for yourself rather than just execute what your boss wanted done," Jeff added.

"Right. I was told what the objective was, and I was given quite a lot of freedom on how to get it done. I could bring my brains to work."

"My guess is that you also were accountable for the outcome."

"Oh, yes. I knew what had to be produced, by when, and at what cost. I was accountable. We all were."

"The result?" Jeff asked.

"It was wonderful! I did some of the best work of my career as a part of that group," Debbie said with a broad grin.

"How did you feel while the project was in progress?"

"The work was hard, and we were putting in a lot of overtime. We were tired, but we were energized. I remember my supervisor coming to one of our late-night meetings. She brought pizza for all of us and told us how proud she was of the work we were doing. She reminded us that this project was going to make a difference."

"I thought so. You felt *valued and appreciated*," Jeff said, emphasizing the last three words.

"Yes, I don't think I ever stopped to think about it, but I did. We all did. The work mattered to the organization, and it mattered to us." As Debbie thought about this, she became curious. "How do you know so much about our project?"

"I don't know anything about your project. But I do know some of the principles for engaging people. The projects change, the people change, but the principles don't. When leaders realize in the long run that they work for their people, these things get done."

Debbie studied the list and considered the points Jeff had raised. "I'm afraid that I don't provide these things for my people often enough," she said, thinking out loud.

"But you do know what you need to provide. I have confidence that you will do the things necessary to help your people enjoy the same positive experience you described to me."

"Thanks! Your confidence means a lot to me. I just need to work on ways to engage their heads and hearts, not just their hands," Debbie offered.

"Exactly!" said Jeff.

"I think I get what you mean by Engaging Others. But what about Developing Others?"

"It's pretty straightforward," Jeff responded. "The best leaders invest in the development of their people. Lesser leaders don't."

"What does it look like to develop others?" Debbie asked.

"It can take many forms," said Jeff. "Developing others involves creating the expectation for learning and growing; creating training and development opportunities; providing educational resources—"

"And mentoring!" interjected Debbie.

"Yes, even mentoring," said Jeff. "You may want to continue exploring this topic in your Personal Development Plan for next year," he added.

Debbie made a quick note about a Personal Development Plan. Not only did she not have one, but she wasn't even sure what one would look like.

"Do you have any parting questions for me to think about this next month?" she asked, pen poised.

"I do," said Jeff. He spoke slowly and deliberately so that she could get it all down.

- How much time do you invest looking for talented people to join our organization?
- What are the key characteristics you look for in the people you select?
- To what extent have you successfully engaged each member of your team?
- What are ten specific things you could do to engage individuals more effectively in the work of the team and the organization?
- What have you done to suggest to them that when it comes to Heads Down implementation activities, you work for them?
- How are you encouraging the development of your people?

"I'll get to work on these right away," Debbie said. "This is really helping me, and I believe I'm making progress."

"I know you are. I'll see you in a few weeks. If you have any questions along the way, give me a call."

At home that night, John was intrigued to hear about Engaging and Developing Others. He posed quite a few questions to Debbie about how she might apply these concepts in her situation.

"Thanks for helping me think this through," she said. "By the way, Jeff made a reference to something called a Personal Development Plan. What is that, exactly?"

John shrugged. "I'm not sure, but it sounds like a good thing to have. Maybe it's time to visit the library again."

"Good idea," said Debbie.

An Insight with Impact

As the new week began, Debbie looked at the world differently. She had a new-hire interview scheduled for Tuesday. This time she asked Human Resources to give her two meetings with the candidate and to schedule ninety minutes for each session—not her usual thirty minutes. Following Jeff's lead, Debbie prepared a short list of references for the candidate. She knew that some of the people might not give her an entirely positive reference, but she wanted to be up front and honest.

At the end of her first meeting with the candidate, Debbie said, "Thank you for your time today. If you are still interested in the job, I want you to come back for another meeting. I know this is a major decision for both of us, so next time, I want you to interview me. Ask anything you like. Also, I've prepared a short list of personal and professional references for you. You may call them if you like, but you are under no obligation. I have to be honest with you, though. Some of these people may not have the most glowing things to say about my past leadership. But I am committed to becoming a great leader, and I see it as a journey. This team is going to do amazing things, and you may be one of the people to help us."

The candidate looked amazed. "Never in my life has a potential employer given me references," she said. "I appreciate your candor." Silently she thought, *I'll prepare interview questions and call the references. But I already know we could easily work together.*

Later that afternoon Debbie entered the library and searched out the librarian. "Hello again," Debbie called to her.

The librarian looked up and a smile of recognition crossed her face. "Hello," she replied.

"I'm afraid I don't know your name," said Debbie.

"It's Jill," the librarian replied. "What can I help you with today?"

"I want to learn more about development plans for people."

"Ah, yes," said Jill. "Sometimes they're called Personal Development Plans and other organizations call them Individual Development Plans, or IDPs. We have several good references that will help you learn more." Jill pointed Debbie in the right direction and asked, "What else can I do to serve you today?"

At that moment Debbie remembered Jeff's comment that great leaders were always looking for talented people to join their organizations. She had never been on the lookout for people before. She had always relied on HR to send her whoever they could find. However, over the weekend Debbie had answered one of the questions Jeff had given her about Engaging and Developing Others: *What are the key characteristics you look for in the people you select?* Her list included a willingness to serve, a warm personality, a sharp mind, and good communication skills. She was standing face-to-face with a person who seemed to match that profile.

"Jill, have you ever considered a career change?"

"As a matter of fact, I have. I just haven't found the right position in the right company."

"What would you think about joining my team?" Debbie asked.

"Doing what, exactly?"

"Doing what you do here."

"Helping people find resources?"

"You're partially right—helping people. We do sell a product, but our passion is serving people. You seem to get a great deal of satisfaction from that."

"I do," Jill acknowledged.

"Let me get you an application. We do have a process we would need to follow. But I want you to know that it's not about convincing you that you should work for us. It's about us determining together if it makes sense for you to join our company. We're interested in finding a great fit for people. If we can't, we would rather part as friends and have you work somewhere else. So are you still interested?" Debbie asked hopefully.

"Yes, definitely! Now, let's see . . . your question was about development plans."

Debbie walked out the library door an hour later with several books, a couple of articles, and an outstanding template she could use to create her own Personal Development Plan. Not to mention a lead on a valuable new team member.

Back at the office, Debbie began to work on Engaging and Developing Others. Recruiting was part of the mix, and she felt good about her conversation with Jill, but she knew she needed to engage her existing staff. Her upcoming team meeting would be a good place to start.

Although Debbie had already gotten some input from each member of the team regarding Jeff's questions about the future, this would be their first meeting since Debbie reinstated the team. Naturally, she expected some skepticism from the members of the group.

"I'm glad to have you all back together," Debbie said as the meeting began. "I have a confession to make. I made a mistake. I should not have canceled our team meetings. If we're going to get to where we want to go, we're only going to make it by working together."

Charles raised his hand.

"Yes, Charles," said Debbie.

"Where is it, exactly, that we want to go?"

For a moment Debbie froze. Then she remembered how thoughtfully Jeff had responded to all her queries.

"That's an outstanding question," she responded with a smile. "Let's talk about that."

This initiated what was perhaps the most productive conversation the group had ever had. Debbie listened to the input of the group and shared her views along the way. By the end of the meeting, they all had a pretty good idea of what they wanted the future to look like. The group decided to pursue a bold goal—to move from 'Worst to First!' and create raving fan customers of both their salespeople and the clients. That would be their compelling performance challenge for the months ahead. "Raving fan customers will brag about us and act like they are part of our sales force," Debbie said.

She concluded the meeting by saying, "I realize we all spend many of our waking hours at work. I want to do all that I can to make it as rewarding and enriching as possible for each of you. At our next meeting, let's think together about how we can accomplish what we talked about here today. Your homework is to begin thinking about obstacles we'll need to overcome and short-term goals we may want to set. Thank you for sharing your heart on these issues. Please call me if you want to discuss any of this before our next meeting."

After their meeting had adjourned, several people stopped to talk to Debbie. They all made positive comments on the meeting. Debbie could feel a fresh energy from the group. *Perhaps this new approach to leadership is working*, she thought.

That night Debbie started on her own home-work—studying the material on Personal Development Plans. As she read, she came across an idea that made a tremendous amount of sense to her. It was common sense, yet she had never thought of it before. It was simple, direct, and profound:

Leverage your strengths.

This idea might not only help me, she thought, *but it could also help every member of my team*. It was time for another meeting with Jeff. Debbie eagerly anticipated the opportunity to tell him all that had transpired.

The first thing Debbie said when she arrived at Jeff's office was, "I realize that today we should be talking about the *R*, and I really do want to learn about it. But I've got so much to tell you that it may have to wait until our next meeting. Would you mind?"

Jeff was pleased with her enthusiasm. "It's your meeting. Where do you want to begin?"

She told him about the team meeting, the progress they were making, and how Jill would be a perfect addition to the team.

Jeff could tell by her energy level and the things she was sharing that she was beginning to get it.

"What can I do to help?" he offered.

"Tell me if I'm on the right track. I was doing some research about Personal Development Plans, and I came across an idea that struck me like a bolt of lightning. As you know, I've always thought I had to 'fix' people. Based on what I've been reading, I would rather 'fit' people in the right jobs and help them leverage their strengths, rather than 'fixing' them later. If this idea is right, it would change the way I do things. What do you think?"

"That's another breakthrough for you as a leader," Jeff said with a smile. "Many leaders never get that one. They spend their entire career trying to make people do things they are not naturally gifted or inclined to do. That's why it's so important to engage the right people. Changing people—or 'fixing' them, as you put it—is very hard to do."

Jeff continued, "Let me add that people can learn new skills, and people can enhance their existing abilities. This can happen even outside a person's natural strengths. That's why we believe training is essential. But the purpose of training isn't to try to 'fix' people. I heard a great saying years ago: 'No matter how long the runway, that pig ain't gonna fly.' Many leaders invest a tremendous amount of time, energy and money to give flying lessons to people who will never fly. As leaders, we must be willing to accept the fact that there are some things that certain individuals will never learn to do well. And that's okay."

"So—?" Debbie thought she had learned something, but she was not quite sure of its significance.

"So I'm going to quote Peter Drucker again: 'The leader's objective is to leverage the strengths of people and make their weaknesses become irrelevant.'"

"Help me with the day-to-day implications of that," Debbie said.

"Okay, let's start with a question. Do you have any people on your team who are struggling?"

"Yes. Charles has had trouble ever since he arrived. I worked side by side with him for a couple of days, but, to be honest, it didn't seem to help."

"You may need to work with him to discern the answer to the 'fit' question. What are his strengths? Do they match the role? Is he in the right role? If you think he's in the right spot, you'll need to ask some additional questions. Was he properly trained? Does he clearly understand his responsibilities?

"Once you're convinced the fit is right for each position, development can smooth rough edges, close any gaps that may be holding the individual back, and even prepare him or her for future opportunities. All of this is possible if the person is in the right job. Helping people leverage their strengths is one of the most rewarding parts of the leader's role."

I knew this was big, Debbie thought. She also knew that a

Helping people leverage their strengths is one of the most rewarding parts of the leader's role.

conversation with Charles could be very insightful. She jotted down a note to schedule a meeting with him as soon as possible.

"Thanks, Jeff. You helped me understand how and why leveraging strengths is critical. Even though we didn't talk about R, I've already got my homework assignment."

"What's that?" Jeff asked.

"I'm going to meet with Charles and see how I can help."

How Can It Be Better?

The next morning, Debbie called Charles to schedule a meeting. They agreed to meet at 3:00 p.m. the following day. She explained that her primary objective was to help and that to do that, she needed to understand his situation completely.

When she approached his office at the appointed time, she was anxious but optimistic. She believed that this conversation would help her help him. She wanted him to enjoy his work, and she wanted him to be successful.

It turned out to be a very productive meeting. Debbie did an effective job of framing the issue. She asked open-ended questions and listened carefully. Although they didn't reach any definitive conclusions, Charles fully embraced the idea of leveraging his strengths. He admitted that he didn't have complete clarity on his strengths as they applied to his job as a project manager. He committed to think about that. At the same time, Debbie realized that she could help Charles by providing more training and direction.

It seemed to both of them that they had made progress. They agreed to meet again the following week to continue their discussion.

Debbie realized that she was doing more and more of the things great leaders do. She was helping her team formulate a compelling vision that they wanted to pursue, and she was investing a greater percentage of her time assisting them as they worked to achieve their goals. She was also working to get the right people on the team and fully engage those who were already with her. She found her redefined role as team leader to be thoroughly enjoyable. People were responding and results were improving. She was looking forward to giving Jeff a full report.

The day arrived for her next meeting with Jeff, and Debbie was ready.

"Good morning, Jeff."

"Morning, Debbie."

Before she was even seated, she said, "I need to know the rest of the secret. I feel like I'm just barely staying ahead of my team on this thing. Let's look at the R today, okay?"

Jeff smiled. He was pleased with her sense of urgency. "Did you do your assignment?"

"Yes, I had a very good meeting with Charles. I'll keep you posted. If the rest of the SERVE model does as much good as the first two parts, there's no limit to what we could accomplish!"

"You realize what you've discovered, don't you?"

"I think so," Debbie said, thinking about it for the first time. "The power of effective leadership."

"You're right—the power of leadership fueled by a passion to serve others. Don't forget to always challenge yourself with the question."

"What question is that?" Debbie asked.

"Am I a serving leader or a self-serving leader? The right answer to that makes all the difference in the world." Jeff paused for a moment to allow that thought to linger in her mind. "Okay," he continued, "what do you think the *R* stands for?"

"I've been thinking about that. Here are my guesses: Rally the troops? Reenergize the organization? Remember the Titans? Really try harder?"

Jeff grinned. "All good guesses, but you struck out." He walked over to the whiteboard and wrote just two words next to the *R*.

S ee the Future

E ngage and Develop Others

R einvent Continuously

V

E

"**Reinvent Continuously**," Debbie read. "Those sound like buzzwords from a consultant."

"That might be, but it's the best language I've found to describe the behaviors it encompasses. I've heard other phrases used: creative dissatisfaction, a healthy disrespect for the status quo, continuous improvement, and so on. Although all of these are great concepts, none of them seems to capture all that Reinvent Continuously does. Besides, none of them starts with an *R*."

Debbie laughed and added, "I think the model would lose something if it were spelled SECVE or SEDVE!"

"You're right!" Jeff said with a chuckle.

"So how should I apply this idea on a day-to-day basis?" Debbie asked.

"This is a big concept. And it has a tremendous impact on what great leaders do. To help explain it, I've broken it down into three components."

"I'm ready," Debbie said as she flipped her notebook open to a blank page.

"First, great leaders Reinvent Continuously on a personal level. They are always interested in ways to enhance their own knowledge and skills. The very best leaders are learners. Great leaders find their own approach to learning—some read, some listen to tapes, some spend time with mentors. They do whatever it takes to

If you stop learning, you stop leading.

keep learning. I believe this to be true: If you stop learning, you stop leading."

Debbie thought for a moment. "Why is learning so critical to the leader? It seems like once you know how to do your job, you could devote your time and attention to more important matters."

"There are several reasons. One is that the leader must model the behavior he or she wants people to emulate. If I'm not serious about personal reinvention, you can bet the majority of my people will not be, either.

"Another reason learning is critical is survival. We must all learn to Reinvent Continuously to keep up with our competitors and the rate of change in our world.

"Next is the reality that many of the answers that worked in the past are not working today. We must have fresh, innovative thinking and new ideas to prepare adequate responses to the challenges our organization faces.

"And, finally," Jeff said, "if all that is not enough, I believe that personal reinvention should be one of a leader's highest priorities because we have a stewardship responsibility to maximize our God-given talents. We can only do that as we continuously learn and grow. It's one way we leverage our strengths as we discussed in our last meeting."

"All right," said Debbie with a smile, "you convinced me."

"The second part of Reinvent Continuously applies to systems and processes. Great leaders are

always seeking answers to questions like these:
How can we do the work better? How can we do
it with fewer errors? How can we do it faster?
How can we do it for less? Leaders must also work
to instill the desire for improvement into the people
doing the day-to-day work. The leader may cham-
pion this cause, but the people make it happen—
or not."

"Our team needs to ask those questions," Debbie
observed. "Our results have improved slightly over
recent months, but they are not close to where they
need to be."

"I think these questions, and others like them,
will serve your team well during the planning
process," Jeff said. "Keep in mind that as a leader,
you want to ask these questions all the time.

"The third part of Reinvent Continuously is
the idea of structural reinvention," Jeff continued.
"Many people assume that an organizational structure is permanent. In many cases, the organizational
structure no longer serves the business—the people
are serving the structure. Great leaders don't change
the structure just for something to do. However,
they understand that their organizational structure
should be fluid and flexible. Other, less proficient
leaders tend to let the structure drive their decisions
rather than adapting the structure to meet the ever-
changing demands of the business."

"Reinvent Continuously is a big concept,"
admitted Debbie. "I think I've got a lot of work
to do on this one."

"You've already started. You're working on your development plan—that's reinventing on a personal level. You're asking your team how they can change the work processes to improve performance. And, finally, you reinstated the team because you felt that it would provide a better structure to accomplish what needs to be done. I think you're well on your way!"

"I appreciate your vote of confidence," Debbie said. "I'm trying. Do you have any questions for me to think about on this topic?"

"You bet. Here are a few."

- Who are your mentors?
- What are you reading or listening to on tape?
- What systems or processes in your area of responsibility need to be changed to enhance performance?
- How could the areas under your leadership be structured differently to enhance performance?

"Thanks, Jeff," Debbie said as she finished jotting down the questions. "Your insights and encouragement mean more to me than you'll ever know. As always, I'm looking forward to our next meeting."

What Is Success?

Back in the office, it was apparent that morale was on the upswing. Debbie was hopeful that performance would follow. She was still listening as much as possible. She was still actively looking for little ways to serve her team. She was delegating more often, and that allowed her more time to think about the future. She was scouting for talent, rather than just waiting for HR to send her warm bodies. She was investing more time in the interview process, and she was working purposefully to engage the hearts and heads of her people.

At times, it all seemed overwhelming. But in her heart Debbie knew that she was just laying the foundation for bigger and better things. As she prepared for the upcoming team meeting, she really wanted to engage the team in Reinventing Continuously. So she sent an e-mail.

Send to:	Team 7
From:	Debbie
Subject:	Upcoming Meeting
Date:	March 1
Action Requested:	See Below

As you prepare for our next team meeting, please try to identify at least one thing we currently do in this department that you believe we could eliminate with few or no ill consequences. If we are going to accomplish all that we discussed at our last meeting, we must eliminate anything that is not adding significant value to our customers, our team, or our organization. I look forward to hearing your ideas!

This should get the reinvention wheels turning, she thought. And it did.

Debbie began the meeting by introducing the idea of Reinventing Continuously. She challenged the group to begin immediately to eliminate work that had diminished in value. She committed her best efforts to help them improve the work process to make things better, faster, and lower in cost to the organization.

People were reluctant to share in the beginning, because they were still suspicious about Debbie's motives. But slowly, one after another, the team members began to offer their ideas. Glenda suggested eliminating one of the monthly reports she produced. She said she wasn't sure how many people used it, and besides, everyone had the information on his or her laptop computer. When Debbie asked the group what they thought, people agreed. Most did not use the report, and the few that did said they had never thought about the data being available on their laptops.

In an attempt to manage people's expectations and minimize disappointment, Debbie explained that while it might not be possible for every idea to be adopted, the discussion would still be very healthy. By the end of the meeting, the group had accepted seven of the dozen ideas that had been shared.

Next, they moved on to discussions about the upcoming year. Debbie took a blank sheet of flip chart paper and hung it on the wall. "This is the current state of our plan for the year," Debbie said.

Charles commented, "It's blank."

"Yes, and that's the whole point! We get to create a plan that will help us reach our goals of creating raving fan customers of our sales folks and clients—starting with a blank sheet."

That led to a very productive debate about goals, strategies, and tactics. The question that seemed to inspire the most energy was "What will we need to do differently to significantly improve our service next year?"

After the meeting, Debbie had individual conversations with members of the team about their current work and the upcoming year. Many of these conversations led to improvements in the department. Several team members asked Debbie whether a portion of the next planning meeting could be devoted to solving some current work issues. She thought that was a wonderful idea. She had been so focused on the future, she had forgotten about letting the team manage the present. Debbie remembered the Heads Up–Heads Down discussion with Jeff. She quickly amended the next meeting agenda to include time to work on current issues.

Before Debbie knew it, it was time again for her meeting with Jeff. She looked forward to telling him how her team had begun to reinvent their work by eliminating things that didn't add value. She also wanted to tell him about Jill, who was going to join her team in a few days.

When Debbie arrived at Jeff's office, he had several stacks of computer printouts spread out on his table.

"What are you working on this morning?" Debbie asked with a smile.

"I'm just trying to stay in touch with the performance of the various units," Jeff said. "I notice your team's performance has improved."

"Yes, but we've got a long way to go."

"Congratulations on your progress. I think it ties in nicely with what we're going to talk about today."

"Are we going to address the V?" Debbie asked.

"Yes, we are. Today we're going to talk about success."

"Success?" Debbie looked puzzled. "Help me connect success with a V."

"These days, many people are confused about what success is. This is often fueled by everyone's desire to see quarterly earnings. Don't get me wrong—earnings are absolutely essential. But I think there is more to success than that."

"What do earnings and success have to do with the *V*?"

Jeff turned and wrote on the whiteboard.

See the Future

Engage and Develop Others

Reinvent Continuously

Value Results and Relationships

E

"The *V* stands for **Value Results and Relationships**," he explained. "Great leaders— those who lead at a higher level—do both. Both are critical for long-term survival. Not either/or but both/and. For too long, many leaders have felt that they had to choose. Most corporate leaders have said it's all about results."

"In reality, there are two tests of a leader. Do they get results? And do they have followers? By the way, if you don't have followers, it's very hard to get long-term results."

Profits and financial strength are the applause we get for a job well done.

"The way to maximize your results as a leader is to have high expectations for both results and relationships. If we can take care of our customers and create a motivating working environment for our people, profits and financial strength are the applause we get for a job well done. You see, success is both results and relationships. It's a proven formula."

Debbie nodded in agreement.

"Debbie, I saw on your application that you played on a highly competitive volleyball team in college."

"Yes, we made it to the national tournament twice."

Jeff could hear the pride in her voice. "Who was your coach?"

"Joan Hammond."

"I don't know her, but I bet I can tell you something about Ms. Hammond. She expected results, and you had a good relationship with her, didn't you?"

Debbie beamed. "You're right. She was very demanding, and we knew we were supposed to produce results. But we loved her, too."

"For your team to be as good as you obviously were, it is highly probable that Ms. Hammond was an outstanding leader. Leaders of her caliber provide both challenge and support. They expect results and have very good relationships with those they wish to lead."

"We would do whatever she asked us to do. We trusted her leadership. But that was just a sport. As a leader in the business world, how do I demonstrate that I Value Results and Relationships?" Debbie asked.

"The same way Ms. Hammond did. How did you know she valued results?"

"There were a lot of ways, I guess. I never really thought about it. She had high expectations, and we had clear goals. There was a high level of accountability, and we worked hard to solve the problems that were negatively affecting our performance. Plus, we had great parties to celebrate our successes."

"Exactly! Your coach knew that all these things communicated clearly that she valued results."

"Those are things I already do to some degree, but I can certainly improve in each of those areas," Debbie admitted.

"How about on the relationship side? How did you know that she valued relationships?"

As Debbie began to offer her thoughts, Jeff wrote them on the whiteboard.

"Ms. Hammond was a great listener," Debbie noted.

"Good, what else?" Jeff prodded.

"She always seemed to make time for us. She cared deeply about each of us as individuals. She also appreciated our efforts."

"So she accentuated the positive?" Jeff asked.

"Yes. I've heard it described as 'catching people doing things right.'"

"Anything else?"

"Probably, but those are the things that come immediately to mind." When Jeff finished writing, they looked at Debbie's list:

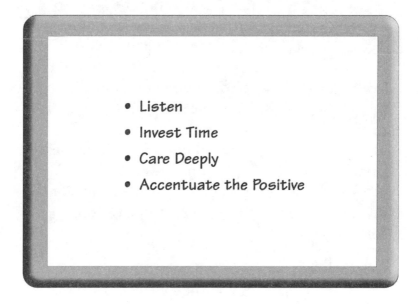

- Listen
- Invest Time
- Care Deeply
- Accentuate the Positive

"That's a good list," Jeff said. "It probably covers the basics of what a good relationship involves.

However, there's one important thing to keep in mind as you work to build and nurture significant relationships. Although we all have a lot in common, people are different. Each person has his or her own personality and temperament. Building meaningful relationships can never be reduced to a checklist of activities. If your heart is right and your motives are valid, most people will meet you halfway when establishing relationships. It's one more thing you, as a leader, must always be aware of.

> **"People will not give you their hand until they can see your heart."**
> **—John Maxwell**

"Valuing relationships is important," Jeff continued. "John Maxwell says that 'people will not give you their hand until they can see your heart.' This will require your ongoing attention."

"I'm willing to give it my best effort," said Debbie.

"Great! I'd like to suggest some questions for you to think about that pertain to today's topic."

- How much emphasis do you place on getting results?
- How many of your people would say that you have made a significant investment in their lives?

- What are the ways you have expressed appreciation for work well done in the last thirty days?

Debbie was both enthusiastic and grateful. "Once again, Jeff, you've stretched my thinking."

"I'm glad! Call me if there's any way I can help you before our next meeting."

How's Your Credibility?

Planning was now in full swing, and everyone was involved in the process. The members of the team had decided that some of the performance issues they wanted to work on couldn't wait, so they called a special meeting and determined what they could do to attack those problems immediately. Debbie was proud of them. The initiative was refreshing, and the idea of the team solving a performance problem was amazing. To top it all off, performance continued to improve.

Debbie wanted her team to know how much she appreciated their efforts, so she decided to take them all out to lunch. She had never done this before, but it felt like the right thing to do. They all shared their favorite childhood memories while they waited for the food to arrive. This was Jill's idea. She said she wanted to get to know more about people than she would typically learn at work. This was just one more reason Debbie felt good about hiring Jill. She could help Debbie and the entire group with the Valuing Relationships idea. She was a natural. It was obvious that she loved people and people loved her. This realization prompted Debbie to invite Jill out to lunch again a few days later.

"Thanks for coming to lunch with me today."

"My pleasure," Jill replied warmly.

"How is the transition from the library to corporate America going?"

"It's been very smooth. Everyone's been wonderful. I like the work, and the lighting is much better in my new office!"

Debbie laughed. "I always wondered if it was my imagination or not, but most libraries do seem dark to me."

After they ordered lunch, Debbie asked, "Is there any way I can help you in your work?"

Jill replied, "I can't think of anything right now. I'm just so appreciative that you asked me to join your team. Is there anything I can do for you?"

"Since you asked," Debbie said hesitantly, "there is one thing. I've noticed that you have connected immediately with most of the team."

"Yes, they're wonderful people. They've all been extremely helpful."

"You said something at lunch the other day. You said you wanted to get to know people beyond who they are at work and what they do there."

"Yes, I remember saying that. Is that a problem?" Jill asked.

"No, not at all. What you're doing is great. I've gotten some coaching that I need to work harder to help people understand that I Value Results *and* Relationships. It seems as though I still focus most of my energy on getting results."

"So how can I help?" Jill asked.

"I'm not sure. You just seem like a natural when it comes to connecting with people. I don't have any specific request. It's just that—" Debbie hesitated, trying to put her thoughts into words. "If you have any advice for me about relationship skills, I would appreciate your help. I know my heart's in the right place. I just can't seem to express my feelings."

"I don't have any immediate ideas, but if I think of something, I'll let you know."

They had a great time together. Debbie could sense that a long-term friendship could be in the making.

As they walked back to the office, Jill said, "I do have one idea for you."

"What's that?" Debbie asked.

"Just do what I've started doing. Find out about people's lives outside work. What are their goals and dreams and struggles? Take today, for example. When we sat down at lunch, you asked me if you could help me with anything at work. Why not say, 'Is there anything I can help with?'—period? Maybe someone needs help outside work, and if you asked, that person might let you into his or her world.

Someone told me something a long time ago that makes a lot of sense: 'People don't care how much you know, until they know how much you care.'"

"Thanks, Jill. You've sure given me something to think about."

Over the next week Debbie did think about Jill's advice. Taking an interest in people's personal lives felt weird to her—not quite right. So she decided to ask Jeff about it. Their meeting was still a week away, but he had suggested several times that she call if she had questions. She called his assistant and scheduled a ten-minute phone meeting with Jeff for the following afternoon.

She called promptly at 3:00 P.M. as planned.

"Hi, Jeff. It's Debbie. I have a question I thought you could help me with."

"Sure, what is it?" Jeff asked.

"I'm still working hard on valuing relationships, and I want your opinion on something. How concerned should I be about what a person does outside the office?"

If success is about results and relationships, you'll have to take a few relational risks along the way.

"Tell me more," Jeff said, not quite sure what Debbie really wanted to know.

"I want people to know that I really do care about them, so should I get involved in their personal business—what they like to do in their off time, their personal goals, their past?"

"I think I understand the question. You want to know if you can be their friend and their coworker."

"Not their coworker—their boss!" Debbie said.

"Okay, I get your point. It goes back to how you, as a leader, define success. If success is about results and relationships, you'll have to take a few relational risks along the way. Under this definition of success, you have to be able to say to Sally or Steve or whomever, 'I want to have a personal relationship with you, and you still have to fulfill the expectations of your role within the company.' I believe both are possible."

Jeff continued, "Can you be the best of friends with every member of your team? Probably not. However, you can have a meaningful, personal relationship with each one of them."

"But how do you do that?" Debbie asked.

"Here's one thing I did with my direct reports in my previous company to foster our relationships. This may not be right for you—and timing is important—but when we began our annual planning a couple of years ago, I sat down with each individual and looked at his or her plans and goals for the year. I said, 'I am going to help you execute this plan and achieve these goals—that's what I'm paid to do. But I want to help you in other ways as well.'"

Jeff could sense Debbie's hesitation in the silence on the other end of the line.

"And most of them got as quiet as you just did. They had no idea what I was talking about. Here's what I said. 'I don't know how I can help you beyond the plans and goals you've just outlined, but if you'll share with me things that you would like to accomplish in your life outside work, I'll help any way I can.'

Jeff elaborated. "I told them that if they would share with me the top five things they wanted to Be, Do, Have, and Help in their lifetime, I would do all that I could to assist them in achieving those twenty things."

"Did they tell you what they really wanted?"

"Not all of them—not at first, anyway. However, over about a two-year period, I guess all of them did."

"Give me an example of what someone might put on their list."

"Gladly. One man said he wanted to *be* a great father. When I heard a CD on the topic that I thought he might like, I sent him a copy.

"Someone indicated that one thing they wanted to *do* was to attend the Masters golf tournament in Augusta. It was only a few months until I was able to get her tickets for the event.

"Another person said she wanted to *have* a more balanced life. We looked at the issue together. We started by defining what a balanced life might look like from her perspective. Then we identified some specific things we could both do to help her move in that direction. It also gave us something we could monitor on an ongoing basis. I haven't worked with that woman in about two years, but just last week I sent her a new book that I thought might help her as she continues her journey.

"Finally, a member of my previous team expressed the desire to *help* homeless people in our city. I happened to be on the board of another company with the chairman of the downtown homeless center. I was able to introduce them.

"That's so generous of you," Debbie said.

"I want to invest in the lives of my people. I can't help all of them with everything on their individual lists, but I can usually do something. That's one way I can demonstrate the fact that I value relationships. Does that help you with your question?"

"Yes, thank you. I'll see you next Thursday."

"I'm looking forward to it!"

As she hung up the phone, Debbie thought about how Jill's instincts were correct. *I do have much more latitude than I thought in this relationship arena. I'll have to keep working on it.*

The next meeting with Jeff came up quickly. The first thing he wanted to know was what she had been thinking regarding Value Results and Relationships.

Debbie replied, "I think I can nail the results part. I'm still thinking about how to value relationships. I'm trying to listen better and take time to build relationships. I don't think I'm ready to ask my team the type of questions we discussed on the phone. I'm not sure they're ready for that, either. I'll probably start with Jill and see how that goes. Maybe at some point in the future, I'll try the deeper questions with the whole team."

"That's probably wise. As I said when I shared that idea, you have to get a sense of when the time is right. You know, I couldn't have done that exercise with my people early in my career."

"Why not?" asked Debbie.

"I was not a serving leader. Unfortunately, I was a self-serving leader. You may decide not to talk to your people about these things and that may be right for you at this time. But in my case it wasn't a timing issue; it was a heart issue. I would never have even thought of asking those type of questions because life was not about them—*it was all about me.* I'm not proud of it, but I'm thankful for the experience. I learned some tremendous lessons."

"What changed?" Debbie asked.

"Me," Jeff said with a smile.

"Why did you change? What happened?"

"Someone saw potential in me, invested in my life, and helped me understand that the rewards of becoming a serving leader were far greater than being a self-serving one. I guess you could say I had a change of heart."

"Thanks for sharing that with me," Debbie said. "I feel like my heart is changing, too. Thanks for investing in my life."

"Are you ready for today's topic?" Jeff asked.

"You mean the *E*? Sure."

"Do you know what all legitimate leadership is built on?"

"I don't think I know," Debbie confessed.

"Trust," Jeff said.

"Trust?" Debbie didn't see the connection between trust and the *E*. "*Trust* doesn't start with an *E*," she protested.

You must gain the trust of your people. If you don't have their trust, you'll never be a great leader.

"You are correct. However, as a leader, you must gain the trust of your people. If you don't have their trust, you'll never be a great leader."

"That's a pretty serious statement. Does that mean that I'll never accomplish anything as a leader without the trust of my team?"

"No," said Jeff. "It just means that the group you lead will never reach its full potential if you are not trusted."

"Okay—but what does all of this have to do with the *E*?"

"The *E* stands for **Embody the Values**." Jeff went over and wrote it on the board:

See the Future

Engage and Develop Others

Reinvent Continuously

Value Results and Relationships

Embody the Values

"I'm really confused," Debbie said. "Please connect the dots for me."

"Gladly," Jeff continued. "All genuine leadership is built on trust. There are many ways to build trust. One way is to live consistently with the values you profess. If I say customers are important, my actions had better support that statement. If I choose to live as if customers are not important, people will have reason to question my trustworthiness. And in the final analysis, if I am deemed untrustworthy by my people, I will not be trusted—or followed as a leader."

"Okay," Debbie replied, "I think I know what it means to Embody the Values. My next question is, which values? Are these the values you wrote about in the annual report?"

"Yes and no. My hope is that all of the leaders throughout this organization will communicate our values to their people and integrate them in their areas of influence. One of the things great leaders do is establish, articulate, model and enforce core values."

So what's the 'no' part of your answer?" Debbie asked.

"Embody the Values is a leadership practice that certainly transcends our company, just like all the other practices in the SERVE model. For a leader to be successful, he or she must embody the values of their organization. So, if you are leading at your child's school or in your church, you should embody the values of that particular organization. The power is in the trust and credibility you build, not a specific set of values that represent the 'right' ones."

"That makes a lot of sense. My key take-away is that I had better 'walk the talk' if I want to build and maintain the trust of my staff."

"Yes. Unfortunately, most people stumble the mumble," said Jeff with a smile. "If you don't Embody the Values, you miss an opportunity to shape the culture of the organization, and you do tremendous damage to your own leadership."

"I think I've got it," Debbie offered.

"Good! Can you give me an example?" Jeff asked.

"I'll try. Because one of our values is serving others, if I did not take time to listen to my team members, I would not embody that value because that would be self-serving. If this behavior were to continue over time, my credibility would go down, and, potentially, so would my people's trust in my leadership."

Jeff nodded his approval. "People follow leaders they can trust. If you Embody the Values, you can begin to build the trust you need to lead effectively."

"Thanks! I'll definitely think about living the values. What's my homework assignment for next time?"

"I have a few questions for you to consider. Ready?"

Debbie nodded yes, and he asked her the following questions.

- How can you better integrate our organizational values into how your team operates?
- What are some ways you can communicate our core values to your team over the next thirty days?
- How can you alter your daily activities to create greater personal alignment with these values?
- How can you recognize and reward people who embody these values?

"Thanks, Jeff. Once again, I have a lot to think about."

"Leaders always have a lot to think about, Debbie."

Jeff's response struck a profound chord in Debbie. "Before I go," she said, "I'd like to give you a question to think about prior to our next meeting."

"Great!" said Jeff with a smile. "What is it?"

"I was at a dinner party the other night where the host asked everybody to go around the table and tell the others what two people—past or present—they would love to have dinner with some evening. It got me wondering: Who are the leaders—past or present—who you think best demonstrate the SERVE approach to leadership?"

"That's a fascinating question!" Jeff responded. "I'll have to think about it for a while."

"Okay," said Debbie. "I'll be looking forward to your answers. See you in a few weeks."

Serving Leaders

Debbie became more and more enthusiastic over the next few weeks. She was beginning to see how all of what Jeff was teaching her fit together. As the day of their next meeting approached, she thought about the question she had asked at the end of their last meeting. *I wonder who he'll select as the leaders who best put the principles of SERVE into practice?*

On the morning of their meeting, Debbie headed for Jeff's office with her newfound sense of optimism. *I've learned so much. This mentoring has been a great experience!*

They began by sharing what was going on in their personal lives. From the beginning, Jeff had always expressed interest in her life, both at work and outside the office.

Turning to the business at hand, Jeff asked, "Have you had any fresh insights since our last meeting?"

"Yes, quite a few," Debbie said with some satisfaction in her voice.

"Like what?"

"I learned that the ideas you shared actually work!

Also, as I began to think about establishing and living the values of our organization, I realized that 'if it is to be, it is up to me.'"

"If it is to be, it is up to me."

"Excellent!" Jeff responded enthusiastically.

Debbie continued, "Here's what I mean by that. Not only do I win or lose credibility based on how well I embody the values, but I also set the tone and the example for my team. No one controls how well I do this except me. I guess it's just part of being a leader."

"You've got it. If your heart is right and your head is clear, that should help keep your hands aligned with the values. Thanks for sharing that insight. Anything else we need to cover before we pick up where we left off last time?" Jeff asked.

"I don't think so. Let's go straight to my last question. Who are the leaders—past or present—who you think best put the SERVE behaviors into practice on a daily basis?"

"I gave a great deal of thought to your question," said Jeff.

Debbie was eager to hear who he had in mind. "And?" she prodded.

"One person I thought of was Nelson Mandela. Here's a guy who was wrongly jailed for almost twenty-eight years, yet when he was finally released he wasn't angry. He came out with a desire to serve and help. He even invited his jailers to his inauguration when he was elected president of the Union of South Africa. He had a vision of the future. He gathered people around him that he could develop, and he seemed to be learning all the time, even when he was in jail. Mandela certainly valued people and results, and he lived the values. He really did it all."

"You're right—he's a remarkable man," said Debbie. "You know, somebody similar to Mandela who I'd like to have dinner with someday is Jimmy Carter. I mean, he wasn't considered the greatest president while he was in office, but I think he'll go down as the greatest ex-president of all time. He's created an incredible team to build thousands of homes for the poor through Habitat for Humanity. And he won a Nobel Peace Prize for his work facilitating peace talks in troubled areas of the world. He certainly is modeling a leader who is selfless and willing to serve."

"That's a good one," said Jeff. "I'd love to have dinner with him, too."

"Who else?" Debbie asked.

"You know who came to my mind right away? Jesus of Nazareth."

"Really?"

"Yes," said Jeff. "Here's a leader who selected twelve inexperienced people and developed them into leaders who could carry on after he was no longer there in bodily form. When people asked him questions, his answers always showed a servant heart. 'How do you lead?' 'By following.' 'How can I be first?' 'By being last.' He said that

even he had come to serve, not to be served. He
symbolized his whole philosophy of servant leadership at the Last Supper, where he washed the feet of
the disciples and told them essentially, 'Just as I have
done for you, you must do for others.' He constantly was talking about the future. He engaged his followers. He was continually challenging people to
change not only themselves but also each other and
their organizations. He cared about both people and
results. And he certainly embodied the values."

"That's interesting," Debbie replied. "I doubt
that most people would think of Jesus as a leadership role model. But now that you mention it, his
organization has been around for two thousand
years. I wonder how many Fortune 100 companies
will be around in two hundred years, let alone two
thousand? Jesus might be the greatest servant leadership model of all."

"I certainly think so. So how about you? What
great leader of the past might you want to have dinner with?"

Debbie thought for a minute. "How about
Martin Luther King, Jr.? Of all of the great leaders I
recall reading about, he's one who had a truly powerful vision—a dream that one day people wouldn't
be judged by 'the color of their skin, but by the con-
tent of their character.' He saw the future, engaged
others, and embodied all the other qualities we've
talked about."

"Yeah, Dr. King would be a really good choice."

Debbie saw that their time was nearly up. "Do you have any homework questions for me this week?" she asked.

"No," he replied. "Just study your notes. At our next meeting—which will be our last, you know—we'll spend our time reviewing what we've talked about over the last year or so. You've done well, so it will be a fun session."

Debbie felt pleased by Jeff's compliment and at the same time sad that their sessions were coming to an end.

"This has been an interesting discussion," she said as she headed for the door. "Interesting enough that I'm going to have to give the subject more thought."

Jeff smiled and repeated something she'd heard him say before. "Leaders always have a lot to think about, Debbie."

Let's Review

In the days that followed, Debbie reflected on all the things she'd learned during her meetings with Jeff. She realized that her time with him had made a profound impact on her. It had certainly changed her leadership point of view. She would never look at leadership or her team in the same way again.

The team had a new energy and enthusiasm that truly amazed her. The performance of the group continued to improve. The goals they set around creating raving fan customers were very aggressive, yet everybody felt they were achievable. They all believed they could move from "Worst to First." They decided the key would be twofold: first, unprecedented levels of customer service; second, working together as a team—not independently, as had been their custom.

All of these changes are the result of actions that grew out of my discussions with Jeff, Debbie thought. *He pushed me to become a different kind of leader, and that has made all the difference. I guess it is true: Everything rises and falls on leadership.*

On her way down the hall, she encountered Charles.

"I was just coming to see you," he said. "I want to thank you for all the help you've given me over the past few months. I've decided to move to the catalogue customer call center. I think my strength lies in that area—not in project management. Working side by side with you helped me identify what it took to be a good project manager. Those meetings we had to discuss my strengths really got me thinking. My last day will be in two weeks."

"I've enjoyed our time together, too," Debbie said warmly. "I respect your decision, and I'll miss you."

"By the way," said Charles, "there's a fabulous woman over there who I think would be perfect for my job. I believe she has an appointment with you next week."

"Thanks for recruiting for us," said Debbie with a smile.

Charles said, "One more thing: Thanks for listening."

"Listening?" Debbie asked.

"Yes, I know I shared a tremendous amount of personal stuff during our meetings. I appreciate that."

"If I can help you with anything, Charles, even when you get over to the call center, please let me know."

As she rounded the corner, Debbie ran into Jill.

"Hi, Deb! Looks like you're managing by walking around today!" Jill said with a big smile.

"Never too old to learn new tricks," Debbie replied with a laugh. "By the way," she added, "your customer service and sales feedback scores last month were outstanding."

"Thanks. That's how we're going to go from 'Worst to First!'"

Debbie made her way back to her office. She had cleared her calendar to review her notes from her meetings with Jeff. As she got into it, she realized how helpful the review process was. It crystallized the SERVE model for her. Most important, it organized her thinking so she could teach others what she'd learned.

When Debbie finished the review process, she realized she still had quite a few questions. She didn't panic. Although their last meeting was approaching, Debbie knew that she would always be able to call Jeff with questions.

The morning of their final meeting came soon. Again, Debbie and Jeff spent the first few minutes catching up with each other on personal and family matters. Somewhere along the way, they had become good friends. It wasn't long before the conversation came around to Debbie's review of the SERVE model.

"I started by writing a summary of each component. Would you like to hear what I came up with?"

"Yes, please," Jeff said.

"Okay, here goes. The primary concept is that regardless of their formal title or position, people who want to be great leaders must embrace an attitude of service to others. Leaders can find countless ways to serve the people they lead, and they should always be on the lookout for new and different ways to do this. However, there are at least five critical ways leaders must serve if they want to be as effective as possible.

People who want to be great leaders must embrace an attitude of service to others.

"First, they must be willing and able to See the Future. They must help the people they lead see the destination, as well as the advantages of going there. Everybody needs to see who they are, where they are going, and what will guide their journey."

"Good start," Jeff observed. "What's next?"

"The first E in SERVE stands for Engage and Develop Others. You told me that engaging is a two-part proposition. The first part is to recruit and select the right people for the right job. That means to get the right players on the team. The second part is to do whatever it takes to engage the hearts and the heads of the people. You said that, historically, many leaders have employed the hands and nothing else. That's probably where the term 'hired hands' comes from. We must get much more from people than just their hands."

"You're a great student," Jeff smiled. "What's next?"

"Then there's the *R*—for Reinvent Continuously. This is where our value of creativity can really shine. The leader must be willing to reinvent on at least three levels. The first is personal. Some key questions to ask are, 'How am I learning and growing as a leader?' 'What am I doing to encourage others in my group to constantly learn and reinvent themselves?'

"The second level of reinvention is systems and processes. We must ask ourselves and our people, 'How are we doing the work? How can we do it better? What changes would enhance our ability to serve our customers and each other?'

"And, finally, the third type of reinvention involves the structure of the organization. A good question to ask here is, 'What structural changes do we need to make to be more efficient and effective?' Leaders must always ask these types of questions."

"Continue," Jeff encouraged.

"The *V* is for Value Results and Relationships. I liked the way you said it in the annual report. We value our customers first, and that value guides our behavior and ensures our continuing success."

Jeff quickly added, "What most people don't understand is that they can get better financial results if they have good relationships. We have to raise the value of relationships to a partner of equal importance with results. It's both/and, not either/or."

"I'm beginning to understand that," Debbie acknowledged. "We traditionally teach people the important skills they need to get results: problem solving, decision making, and so on. What I have to continue working on is building relationships and connecting with people—while helping them continually perform better. I've already discovered that we value relationships when we listen to people, invest time with them, care deeply about them, and are recognizing their efforts. I agree with your summary, Jeff."

"Leading at a higher level includes both results *and* relationships," said Jeff with a smile.

Debbie nodded. "The last *E* is Embody the Values. This is fundamental—and ongoing. If we lose our credibility as leaders, our leadership potential will be greatly limited. We must do more than articulate the values, although I believe that is very important. We must not only say it, we must show it."

"Anything else on Embody the Values?" Jeff probed.

"No, I'm still thinking about this one," Debbie said. "I sure don't want to be someone who falls into the trap you warned about—a leader who just 'stumbles the mumble' and doesn't walk the talk."

"I don't think you will," assured Jeff. "Now all you need to do is to figure out how you can help thousands of others learn what you've learned," he said with a smile.

Debbie looked puzzled. "What do you mean 'thousands'?"

"I want you to be the new head of Leadership Development within our organization. If you're open to the idea, I'd like you to start in two weeks."

Debbie was taken aback. "I don't know, Jeff. I still have a lot of questions about leadership. Besides," she jokes, "you haven't put me through the four interviews yet."

"Don't you think all the time we've spent together over the last year counts?" Jeff asked.

"I suppose you're right."

"I know you still have questions, but that means you have humility," said Jeff. "The best teachers are always those who know they haven't got it all figured out."

"I appreciate your confidence in me, but I have a big concern. Who'll lead my team?"

"It sounds to me like you've got a winner in Jill," Jeff said.

Debbie knew at once he was right. Jill would be a fantastic team leader. Yet she still was not yet convinced. "Do I have the credibility to assume such an important leadership position?"

The best teachers are always those who know they haven't got it all figured out.

"You've got all the building blocks to establish your credibility. You've helped turn your team around. And during your time at the company, you have been identified as a person with a tremendous amount of potential. You've got energy, passion, a teachable spirit, and, most important, you've grown into a serving leader. You've got my support and the support of the senior leadership team. This assignment in Leadership Development is just your next opportunity in what I believe will be a long and exciting career."

"Okay, I'll do it!" Debbie said.

"Congratulations!" Jeff extended his hand. "I'll come to your next team meeting and make the announcement."

Passing the Baton

Debbie excelled in her new role overseeing Leadership Development. The extensive notes she had taken during her time with Jeff became the basis of the leadership curriculum. She used the questions Jeff had given her to design thought-provoking assignments that people could use as they applied the principles of SERVE for themselves.

Debbie's team not only completed the year without her but ascended from "Worst to First." They really had created raving fans of both their salespeople and their customers. When Debbie got the news, it was in the form of an invitation from the team to come to a special event to celebrate their achievement.

Debbie showed the invitation to John the moment she got home.

"How does it make you feel that they did this without you?" he asked.

"I feel great about it," she said with a smile.

"Why?"

"By serving them, I helped position them for success. I feel their victory is, in part, my victory."

"You also prepared a successor," John added.

"I sure did. Jill has stepped up and done a wonderful job. I feel terrific about that."

"Are you and Jill still meeting on a regular basis?"

"Yes, we are. We'll meet again next week," Debbie said. "She is now part of our formal mentoring program, and she's my first mentee."

The ability to develop capable successors is a hallmark of great leaders.

"They say that's the final test of leadership," said John.

"What's that?" Debbie asked.

"How your group performs when you're not around. The ability to develop capable successors is a hallmark of great leaders. Ultimately, if your people can't do it without you, you haven't been successful in raising up other leaders."

Remembering what Jeff had said about Jesus and how his disciples had continued to carry his message, Debbie took John's comments as a real compliment.

"Thanks for the support," she said. "I hadn't considered that aspect of leadership before. I thought I was just lucky to have Jill there to step up when I left."

"You may have been lucky. But you also did many things to help Jill and her people win without you."

"Thanks." Debbie gave her husband a hug. "I had a great cheering squad."

A few days later, it was time for the celebration. The word was out about the dramatic performance turn-around of Jill's corporate client services department. Everyone was ready to party. The room was filled with food, balloons, drink, and VIPs—including Debbie's former boss, Tom, and the company president, Jeff.

Jill stood before the crowd and clapped her hands to get everyone's attention. "I know you're all eyeing the great food, but I want to say just a couple of things to the team before we dig in. First, congratulations on accomplishing such a great feat—and something this team will never do again. Never again will we go from 'Worst to First.' We won't have to!"

The room filled with spontaneous applause.

Jill continued, "Second, the reason this happened is because you all did an outstanding job. That really is the bottom line! You lived our core values to the max. You were there for our salespeople and took care of the customers, you served each other, you were great stewards of what we were given to work with, you were creative—very creative—but let's not go into that." People around the room began to laugh at what was obviously an inside joke. "Based on what I can see, next year will be even better."

Again, the crowd applauded.

"Finally, though, we all know that none of this would have been possible without the help, devotion, and unwavering faith of one very special person—Debbie Brewster."

With that, everyone gave Debbie a standing ovation. This was more than she was prepared for. Tears welled up in her eyes as Jill urged her to come forward.

Debbie made her way to the front of the room as Jill held up a gold-embossed plaque.

"On behalf of the entire team, it is my joy and honor to present you with this token of our appreciation for your outstanding leadership."

Through tear-filled eyes Debbie read the words inscribed on the plaque:

> **"Everyone can be great, because everyone can serve."**
>
> —Dr. Martin Luther King, Jr.
>
> *Thank you, Debbie Brewster*
> *For showing us how to serve.*

Acknowledgments

The first people we want to thank are the people who helped create the SERVE model for Chick-fil-A. They are **Lee Burn, Mark Conklin, Cynthia Cornog, Phil Orazi,** and **Tim Tassopoulos.** Their insight, diligence, and hard work were the catalyst for this work. Thank you!

It must also be known that **Truett Cathy, Jimmy Collins,** and the other leaders of Chick-fil-A have field-tested the principles in this book for decades. These men and women have shown the way for countless emerging leaders. They are a real-world testimony to the power and validity of what you have read in this book. Thank you for showing all of us how to SERVE!

We must also thank **Donna Miller, Fran Plunkett, Steve Gottry,** and **Martha Lawrence** for their outstanding efforts and patience as they assisted with the editing, proofing, and rewriting of multiple drafts. They deserve much of the credit for the readability of the final product.

We would also like to recognize some of those who made comments and suggestions along the way through multiple manuscripts. Thanks to **Greg Anderson, Dick Bowley, Bill Dunphy, Jim Fallon, George Flury, Debbie Goins, Nathan Hightower, Thomas Hofler, Jay Kimsey, Rob Martin, Tim Miller, Sonny Newton, Barry Odom, Lee Ross,** and **Beau Sides.**

A number of writers and thinkers have devoted their energy to many of the topics covered in this book. In doing so, they have helped us refine our presentation. Among those we would like to acknowledge here are **Warren Bennis, Bobb Biehl, Sheldon Bowles, Marcus Buckingham, Peter F. Drucker, Robert Greenleaf, Phil Hodges, Bill Hybels, Spencer Johnson, John Maxwell, Michael O'Connor, Andy Stanley, Jesse Stoner,** and **Drea Zigarmi.**

Others who helped in the process are **James Gottry, Linda Purdy, Ginny Van Der Geest,** and **Sjaak Van Der Geest,** production assistants; and **Dottie Hamilt** and **Anna Espino,** Ken's two right hands.

Finally, we want to thank all the people around the world who believe that there is a higher form of leadership—leadership that is not based on power or position; rather, leadership born out of a servant's heart. You are an inspiration for all who know you. Thank you!

—Ken Blanchard and Mark Miller

About the Authors

KEN BLANCHARD

Few people have impacted the day-to-day management of people and companies more than Ken Blanchard. A prominent, gregarious, sought-after author, speaker, and business consultant, Dr. Blanchard is universally characterized by his friends, colleagues, and clients as one of the most insightful, powerful, and compassionate people in the business world today.

From his phenomenal best-selling book, *The One Minute Manager*® (coauthored with Spencer Johnson)—which has sold more than thirteen million copies and remains on best-seller lists—to the library of books coauthored with outstanding practitioners—*Raving Fans*®, *Gung Ho!*®, *Leadership and the One Minute Manager*, *Whale Done!*™, and many others—Ken's impact as a writer is extraordinary and far-reaching. Ken is the chief spiritual officer (CSO) of The Ken Blanchard Companies, an international management training and consulting firm that he and his wife, Dr. Marjorie Blanchard, founded in 1979 in San Diego, California. He is also a visiting lecturer at his alma mater, Cornell University, where he is a trustee emeritus of the board of trustees. Ken is the cofounder of The Center for *FaithWalk* Leadership, which is dedicated to challenging and equipping people to Lead Like Jesus.

Ken and Margie, his wife of more than forty years, live in San Diego. Their son Scott, daughter Debbie, and her husband, Humberto Medina, hold key positions in the Ken Blanchard Companies.

MARK MILLER

A skilled communicator who truly loves what he does, Mark Miller originally joined Chick-fil-A behind the counter of a restaurant as a teenager. He has been a part of the Chick-fil-A corporate staff in Atlanta, Georgia, for more than twenty-five years. He has held several leadership positions within the company, including corporate communications, field (restaurant) operations, and quality and customer satisfaction. Currently he serves as vice president, training and development.

In addition to his work at Chick-fil-A, Mark is active in his local church and is also dedicated to helping develop churches around the globe.

Mark has spoken on numerous occasions at conferences and events in Africa, Asia, Eastern Europe, Central America, and throughout North America.

He is a frequent speaker for the Willow Creek Association, as well as for several other organizations. He is currently partnering with EQUIP to train one million Christian leaders in the international community. Among the wide variety of topics he addresses are leadership, creativity, team building, teaching skills, and evangelism. Mark communicates proven principles with a refreshing pragmatic perspective. His audiences enjoy his energy, his passion, and his bias for action.

Mark and Donna, his wife of more than twenty years, reside in the Atlanta area with their two children.

For more information on Chick-fil-A and its 1,100-plus restaurant locations, please go to its Web site at www.chick-fil-a.com.

Services Available

The Ken Blanchard Companies is a global leader in workplace learning, employee productivity, and leadership effectiveness. Building on the principles of Ken's books, the company is recognized as a thought leader in leveraging leadership skills and recognizing the value of people in accomplishing strategic objectives. The Ken Blanchard Companies not only helps people learn but also ensures that they cross the bridge from learning to doing.

In addition, The Ken Blanchard Companies conducts seminars and provides in-depth consulting in the areas of teamwork, customer service, leadership, performance management, and organizational change.

To learn more about *The Secret*, other books by Ken, or other corporate services, visit the Web site at www.kenblanchard.com or browse the e-store at www.kenblanchard.com/estore. For more information on The Center for *FaithWalk* Leadership, visit www.faithwalkleadership.org or contact:

The Ken Blanchard Companies
125 State Place
Escondido, CA 92029
Phone: (800) 728-6000 or (760) 489-5005
Fax: (760) 489-8407

The Serving Leader
5 Powerful Actions That Will Transform Your Team, Your Business, and Your Community

Ken Jennings and John Stahl-Wert

The Serving Leader argues for an approach to leadership that is both more moral and more effective than the ruthless, anything-for-the-bottom-line approach that has brought disgrace—and often ruin—to many once-mighty organizations. *The Serving Leader* is the most practical guide available to implementing servant leadership.

Hardcover • ISBN 1-57675-265-8
Item #52658 $19.95

Your Leadership Legacy
The Difference You Make in People's Lives

Marta Brooks, Julie Stark, and Sarah Caverhill

If you influence change in the lives of those around you, then you are engaged in an act of leadership. Your leadership legacy is the sum total of the difference you make in people's lives, directly and indirectly, formally and informally. The challenge is how to live in a way that creates a legacy that will make a positive difference in the lives of those around you. *Your Leadership Legacy* shows you how to live a meaningful legacy.

Hardcover • ISBN 1-57675-287-9 • Item #52879 $19.95

The Referral of a Lifetime
The Networking System That Produces Bottom-Line Results... Every Day!

Tim Templeton

The Referral of a Lifetime teaches a step-by-step system that will allow anyone to generate a steady stream of new business through consistent referrals from existing customers and friends and, at the same time, maximize business with existing customers.

Hardcover • ISBN 1-57675-240-2 • Item #52402 $19.95

Berrett-Koehler Publishers
PO Box 565, Williston, VT 05495-9900
Call toll-free! **800-929-2929** 7 am-9 pm EST

Or fax your order to 802-864-7627
For fastest service order online: **www.bkconnection.com**

Empowerment
Takes More Than a Minute
Second Edition

Ken Blanchard, John Carlos,
and Alan Randolph

This book shows managers how to achieve true, lasting results in their organizations. These expert authors explain how to empower the workforce by moving to a supportive, responsibility-centered environment in which all employees have the opportunity and responsibility to do their best.

Paperback • ISBN 1-57675-153-8 • Item #51538 $14.95

Full Steam Ahead!
Unleash the Power of Vision
in Your Company and Your Life

Ken Blanchard and Jesse Stoner

Blanchard and Stoner detail the essential elements of creating a successful vision. In *Full Steam Ahead!* you'll learn to use the power of vision to get focused, get energized, and get great results; create a vision that touches the hearts and spirits of everyone in your organization; and create a vision for your own life that provides meaning and direction.

Hardcover • ISBN 1-57675-244-5 • Item #52445 $19.95

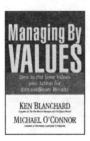

Managing By Values

Ken Blanchard and Michael O'Connor

Based on over 25 years of research and application, *Managing By Values* provides a practical game plan for defining, clarifying, and communicating an organization's values and insuring that its practices are in line with those values throughout the organization.

Paperback • ISBN 1-57675-274-7 • Item #52747 $14.95

Berrett-Koehler Publishers
PO Box 565, Williston, VT 05495-9900
Call toll-free! **800-929-2929** 7 am-9 pm EST
Or fax your order to 802-864-7627
For fastest service order online: **www.bkconnection.com**

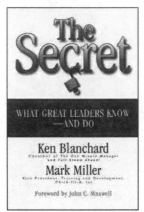